YVES SAINT LAURENT

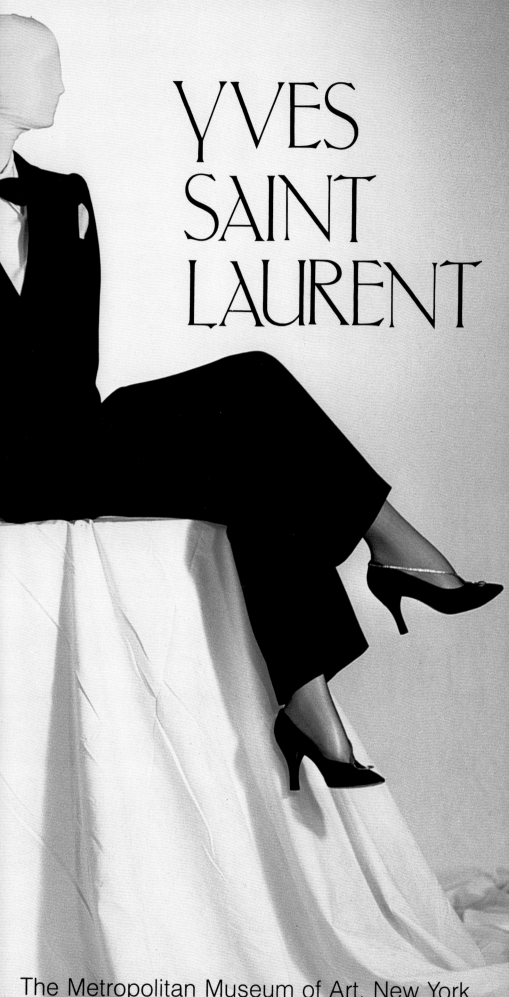

YVES SAINT LAURENT

by

Yves Saint Laurent

and

Diana Vreeland

René Huyghe

Pierre Bergé

Paloma Picasso-Lopez

Marella Agnelli

Catherine Deneuve

Duane Michals

Pierre Boulat

and

Nicholas Vreeland

The Metropolitan Museum of Art, New York

Clarkson N. Potter, Inc./Publishers
Distributed by Crown Publishers, Inc., New York

This book was published in connection with an exhibition at
the Costume Institute of The Metropolitan Museum of Art, New York,
from December 14, 1983, through September 2, 1984.

The exhibition has been made possible by Gustav Zumsteg of Abraham, Zurich.

Copyright © 1983 by The Metropolitan Museum of Art
Published by The Metropolitan Museum of Art, New York

Bradford D. Kelleher, Vice President and Publisher
John P. O'Neill, Editor in Chief
Barbara Burn, Editor
Michael Shroyer, Designer

Type set by Westchester Book Composition, Inc.
Printed by Princeton Polychrome Press and Halliday Lithograph
Bound by Halliday Lithograph

Library of Congress Cataloging in Publication Data
Saint Laurent, Yves.
    Yves Saint Laurent.
    Catalog of the exhibition held at the Costume
Institute of The Metropolitan Museum of Art.
    1. Fashion—History—20th century—Exhibitions.
2. Saint Laurent, Yves. I. Vreeland, Diana. II. Costume
Institute (New York, N.Y.) III. Title.
TT502.S24   1983   746.9′2′0924   83-19409

ISBN 0-87099-360-7 (MMA)
ISBN 0-87099-361-5 (MMA pbk.)
ISBN 0-517-55309-0 (CP)
ISBN 0-517-55310-4 (CP pbk.)

Note: All of the Yves Saint Laurent couture designs shown
in this book are described chronologically in the illustrated
survey beginning on page 89, as nos. 1–218; designs
in color are cited as colorplates 1–70, those in black
and white as figures 1–218.

On the cover/jacket: Yves Saint Laurent with no. 42, "Mondrian" dress;
no. 191, "Matisse" dress; no. 155, "Picasso" dress (Photo Duane Michals)
On the title page: Yves Saint Laurent with no. 69, Evening ensemble;
no. 196, Evening suit (Photo Duane Michals)

Contents

INTRODUCTION

This is the first exhibition the Costume Institute of The Metropolitan Museum of Art has dedicated to the work of one living designer. Why Yves Saint Laurent? Because he is a genius, because he knows everything about women. He lives in a world of artistry, in the sensual life of France, which is still the fashion center of the world. The reason I selected Yves is that for twenty-six years he has kept women's clothes on the same high level. He is followed across the oceans of the world by women who look young, live young, and are young no matter what their age.

For all these years his wide variety of "fatigues"—pants, shirts, boleros, tops, pullovers, coats, and windbreakers—have appeared all over the world, on women in the country, on airplanes, in the street, everywhere. I remember seeing once a young girl in Singapore, with beautiful black Oriental hair and wearing a white Yves Saint Laurent shirt, perched on the back of a motorbike. He is the master of the streets of the world; all of them reveal and radiate his style.

There was a lot of anticipation about his first collection at the house of Dior after Christian Dior died. And when it did appear, in January 1958, there he stood in the window, this boylike angel, with all of the drapers, vendeuses, fitters behind him—so proud—and below him the streets were filled with people thanking God that Paris still remained the fashion center of the world. They didn't stand in the streets for just any hero. Clearly they knew he was a genius and that he would succeed. I wasn't immediately convinced; I felt there was great freshness and style, but I didn't throw out every idea I had about Balenciaga, for instance. When a woman wearing a Balenciaga entered a room, no other woman existed. Her dress was so strong, her appearance so great. There was an authority in that dress, in that woman, which nobody else had. That has never been duplicated, because there is no place for that kind of thing any more. There are no rooms to wear clothes like that in any more. Everything has changed. There is still a lot of money in the world, but it is used in a different way. Social life is different now. There are still beautiful places to wear clothes, but it is quite simple today. And Yves understands this. He lives the way society lives now. You dine at his house, for instance, and you have what you like to eat, what you like to drink—short meals, not too much. That's the way people like to live today. There is no entering a room and knocking them dead. Yves can make a terrific impression, of course; he can do that marvelously. But he's more in the tradition of Chanel. He loves Chanel, who showed modern, emancipated women how to dress, who understood the new century and its changing way of life, its economic and social requirements. Look at the charming navy blue jersey dress with white piqué in figure no. 67; that's a typical Chanel but it's by Saint Laurent! And this is an important point. Both Chanel and Saint Laurent are equalizers. You and I could wear the same clothes; what we have on, *anyone* could wear.

Yves was only twenty-one when he started, which is extraordinarily young for a designer responsible for such an important house as the Maison Dior. But I don't want to dwell on that because I think most genius emerges between fourteen and twenty. If you don't have talent, education can help you to learn and to make a great deal of money, but if you have talent, I don't think education does much for you—only helps light the way. Yves did go to a cutting school for a time, but it's not the people who cut, it's the people who dream and achieve who make the difference.

Yves Saint Laurent has great allure; the whole atmosphere around him has allure. You can never describe allure, it's like a pervading scent; but if you want to know a little about what contributes to Yves' allure, let me tell you what he was like the first time we met, because—and this is important—he hasn't changed. It was before he made a hit with the "trapeze" look when he was at Dior. I met him at his hotel in New York. A thin, thin, tall boy in a thin suit. He was so very young, and not really part of the world. He was something within himself. We were just sort of in each other's company; he didn't tell me anything special and it's still the same way; we have an intimacy of just being in each other's presence and making nothing of it. He struck me right away as a person with enormous inner strength, determination... and full of secrets. I think his genius is in letting us know one of his secrets from time to time.

Yves retains the most extraordinary sweetness. He has a certain quality which very few people have. Like all the very talented, he keeps, he holds, he knows himself. One can easily say that he has innocence. Part of his mysteriousness is that he is like a super child, which has a great effect on people. The people who work for him are very loyal; the house of Saint Laurent is a very happy place, very warm, full of spirit. Saint Laurent has an aura, a presence that many people feel just seeing him or his work, and he really *is* that way... direct, appealing, and true. His image is what he *really* is.

The thought of style disappears when you are in his presence; it's just there, it's what he's got—in himself, his manner, his way of conducting business and friendship. Style is intuitive with him. Yves can draw, he can write, but designing clothes brings everything in him together. That is his métier and he never misses; he does it better with every collection. He is positive about his craft and he is an idealist.

Can you imagine creating four collections a year for twenty-six years? How does he do it? Between collections he does the leisurely things he loves to do—he walks in the desert sunlight of Morocco and on the beaches of Normandy, he listens to music, looks at pictures....

He has a way of opening up in his writing. I remember having been charmed by the extravagance of his language in the few pieces of writing of his I've seen. And it's such a *contrast.* When he talks, you see, it's very simple, it's very concentrated. But when he writes he really gallops through the words! There is equal contrast between his designs for the streets and the elegant and tightly reined extravagance of his designs for the salon.

I like to think that the Maid of France, Jeanne d'Arc, is his real inspiration—young and charming, defiant and brave. Yves has done special things for certain clients—actresses, beauties of great name—but the Maid of France is his real ideal—the young French girl, Jeanne d'Arc or a midinette walking to work in the rain or the spring sunshine in Paris, wearing a shirt and pants.

Girls today look the same all over the world, but they start in the streets of Paris. A girl in America, in Japan, in Germany would rather look like the girls in the streets of Paris than anyone else. The French girls just happen to look wonderful; they are built differently, and in blue jeans, for instance, they look sharp and chic. Yves Saint Laurent has a fifty-fifty deal with the street. Half of the time he is inspired by the street and half of the time the street gets its style from Yves Saint Laurent. His vehicle to the street is *prêt-à-porter*—but behind it all are the superb designs of his couture workroom from which emerged the most beautiful and dashing dresses of the last quarter century. He is without any question the leader in all fashion today.

Follow Yves down the garden path, there's always a pot of gold at the end.

Diana Vreeland
Special Consultant to
the Costume Institute

FASHION AND

THE PSYCHOLOGY OF ART

All art is quintessentially a search for quality, and that very fact makes it an increasingly necessary counterbalance in our society, in which there is a growing tendency to recognize only what can be counted out or measured—the quantitative. Women are more sensitive to this need than men, and for that reason fashion exhibits are, quite fittingly, held in major museums. However, any art form is also revelatory of its creator's psychology—both of his individual psychology which, with the great artists, assumes a prime importance, and of the collective psychology that makes him a part of his society and of his era. In this I include the great fashion designer: his first function is to endow with high quality an article that would otherwise be a mere consumer item. Its creation is revealing of his own personality also, simultaneously reflecting an era and its tastes.

As with any art form, it would be interesting to elaborate a sociology of fashion, as well as an aesthetic, which could then be extended to cover all the practical or decorative arts, architecture as well as furnishings. The creator of clothing unconsciously bears witness to the basic trends of his period and, first and foremost, to its social movement. From his work we can easily decode the predominant class, the social grouping that occupies center stage. Thus, from the Middle Ages to the French Revolution that class was the aristocracy, and its principal aim, its function, was the defense or increase of the territory cultivated by the producing class, the peasantry. Male fashion drew its inspiration from the military uniform: it girded the body. The doublet, for example, molded the torso like a breastplate or a cuirass. As the aristocracy gradually ceased to play the role of warrior and returned to the court, where it was to adopt a luxurious and more ostentatious role, nonfunctional items of clothing took on greater importance and became exaggerated and more purely decorative: lapels, coattails, heels or wigs, trimmings of embroidery or lace. This tendency culminated at Versailles under Louis XIV. The bourgeoisie, in its turn, began its drive to gain power, and the *city* became more important than the *court*—to use La Bruyère's invaluable distinction; clothing became less extravagant and more practical and functional. This trend continued, reaching a climax in the twentieth century. We need only compare the costume of a *maréchal* of France during the Second Empire, with its broad coattails, fancy sash, gold braid, and plumed, three-cornered hat, with that of a modern officer, a de Lattre de Tassigny, who adopted plain battle-dress—in other words a strictly utilitarian garb derived from mechanics' overalls. How significant such transformations! Whereas under the *ancien régime* the regional holiday peasant's costume aped the garb of his lord, from buckled knee breeches to felt plumed hat, in our time the highest military rank tends toward the work clothes of the proletariat! Is there any better way to state the reversal in society, once centered on the aristocracy, then on the nineteenth-century bourgeoisie, today on the worker?

Clothing for women is revealing in yet another way: it is enriched by a woman's appeal, an incarnation both of man's inspiration and of woman's own views about herself. Much more clearly than in the case of male fashion, in female fashion we can observe the compensating ebb and flow of a sensibility that slakes its desires quickly—one that follows a "fashion," one that seeks to refresh its yearnings, to revivify them by shifting to some opposite tendency. Thus, following the last war Dior—and later Saint Laurent—brought in a less formal, more fantastical look, as Chanel had done after World War I, though they did so in a more feminine mode. In their quest for the picturesque—even the exotic—they countered the return to functional logic and sobriety. Here we have the eternal ebb and flow of art, in which sensibilities and perceptions, having been drawn to one polarity, now shift to the opposite end—just as, during this same period, architecture underwent the purification of the Perrets and the even more radical influence of Le Corbusier in reaction to the vegetal exuberance of Art Nouveau. Through the centuries we find this alternation of classic and baroque, but the return to classical purity of form seems to be an especially Latin—and, particularly, a French—characteristic, owing to that people's harmonious and ordered temperament. So fashion—like all the arts—is a doorway through which we can also perceive a psychology of peoples.

René Huyghe, *Académie Française*
(Translated by Richard Miller)

YVES SAINT LAURENT

YVES SAINT LAURENT

I had just blown out the candles of the cake for my ninth birthday when, with a second gulp of breath, I hurled my secret wish across a table surrounded by my loving relatives: "My name will be written in fiery letters on the Champs Elysées."

Our world then was Oran, not Paris. Not Algiers, Camus' metaphysical city of white truths, nor Marrakesh with its benevolent pink magic. Oran, a cosmopolis of trading people from all over, and mostly from elsewhere, a town glittering in a patchwork of all colors under the sedate North African sun. It was a good place to be well off, and we were well off. My summers swept by as if mounted on clouds, at a villa on a beach, where my relatives and friends with similar roots formed an enclave. My father, who owned an insurance business and who was also involved in a few movie productions, was descended from Alsatians who had left Colmar, France, when the Germans took it in 1870. Lawyers, judges, notaries, they had worn the robe of public office. One of my ancestors wrote the marriage contract between Napoleon and Josephine and was made a baron for it. In our baggage there had been a certain civilization and an uprooted prestige. Like colonials elsewhere, like provincials, we maintained a lot of ties to our civilization. There were many lovely dinner parties at our comfortable house in town, and I can still see my mother, about to leave for a ball, come to kiss me goodnight, wearing a long dress of white tulle with pear-shaped white sequins.

My summers always ended too painfully soon. September brought school and the renewal of my anguish. I was different from my classmates, sensitive, shy. I don't intend to recount my whole life, but what I've sketched of the early years are the elements that molded my sensibility. Those years in school traumatized me for life.

"The magnificent and pitiful family of the hypersensitive," Proust wrote, "is the salt of the earth. It is they, not the others, who have founded religions and produced masterpieces." That family is my second family, and whatever I have achieved that might approach a masterpiece I owe to that affiliation as much as to the first. At the time of my early torment, and later when I lay flattened by drugs, anguish, and fear in a military hospital, I did not perceive of mental suffering as a gift. Nor does it seem so each time I begin a collection, even now, four times a year—each time in anguish of not being up to the expectations of the critics, and, more important, not being equal to the task itself, not being able to create, waiting for three

Saint Laurent in his apartment on the rue Babylon in Paris. The painting behind him is by Matisse, whose work has had a great influence on him.

15

weeks out of four for the click that sets my fantasies in motion toward their appointment with the physical world. It doesn't seem a gift, but I know it is. A gift, or a vaccine. I think creative people react to suffering the way they fight death, making the illusions of immortality we call art. "Life," Nietzsche once said, "is not possible without our aesthetic phantoms." And I suppose that, if we are sensitive, suffering teaches us not just the value of things, but a whole scale of values.

Luckily there is a destructive kind of suffering I've never known, the one that comes from lack of recognition. I was seventeen when my drawing took first prize in a fashion contest sponsored by the International Wool Secretariat. I was nineteen when Michel de Brunhoff, who was then editor of French *Vogue*, and who had encouraged me from the beginning, introduced me to Christian Dior. I was immediately hired. Working with Christian Dior was, for me, the achievement of a miracle. I had an endless admiration for him. He was the most famous couturier of the time and had also managed to establish a unique couture house, surrounding himself with out-

Saint Laurent at work in his office at the house of Saint Laurent, on the avenue Marceau. The desk once belonged to his ancestor, a French notary who wrote the marriage contract for Napoleon and Josephine; the ancestor's portrait is visible in the mirror behind Saint Laurent.

standing people. He was a prodigal master and taught me the roots of my art. I owe him an important part of my life and whatever has happened to me since I will never forget the years at his side.

I remember the day Christian Dior, who secretly wished to pull back, told me he wanted me to be more and more involved in the creation of the collections. But for all the admiration I had and have for him I had decided to leave the house soon and take up more seriously my interest in set and costume design. I didn't want to create anonymously—that hasn't worked for creators since the Middle Ages. On the other hand, talented as he was, Christian Dior became a victim of his stardom. His New Look invented instant worldwide fashion, and after that he was under constant pressure to reinvent and reinvent, while Cristobal Balenciaga, for example, was serenely perfecting a style. Balenciaga and Dior were the couture's two great poles of talent when I arrived in Paris. Dior was more brilliant and theatrical, and that counted a lot for me.

In the years since I left that house I've grown more and more wary of fashion, more and more engrossed by style. The achieve-

Yves Saint Laurent surrounded by mannequins and models displaying his "trapeze" collection for the house of Christian Dior, 1958

ment of Gabrielle Chanel has penetrated my sensibility. Fashion is a kind of vitamin for style. It stimulates you, it gets you going. But there's a risk of overdose. It can destroy the balance of your personality—that goes for a designer and also for the woman who wears his clothes. Fashions pass quickly, and nothing is more pathetic than those puppets of fashion outrageously made up one day, pale the next, pleated or ironed stiff, libertine or ascetic. Playing with fashion is an art. The first rule is don't burn your own wings.

When Christian Dior died, the opportunity to do my own collections made me abandon the idea of devoting myself to designing for the stage. At twenty-one I entered a kind of stronghold of glory that's been the trap of my life. I would never lose my love of the theater, but by then Dior had taught me to love something other than fashion and style: the essential nobility of a couturier's craft. I believe that a designer who is not also a couturier, who hasn't learned the most refined mysteries of physically creating his models, is like a sculptor who gives his drawings to another man, an artisan, to accomplish. For him the truncated process of creating will always be an interrupted act of love, and his style will bear the shame of it, the impoverishment. The couture began as a place where the most knowledgeable and most exigent of women were dressed with the greatest perfection. It survives because a few of those women

The 21-year-old Saint Laurent acknowledges the homage of the press from the balcony at Dior after his triumphant first collection.

still survive and because it is subsidized by other activities, such as ready-to-wear collections. In the sixties, when it was clear that a great world of interesting women could not afford couture, I began doing my Rive Gauche *prêt-à-porter*. But I believe that the couture must be preserved at all costs and the term, like a title, protected from debasement. Haute couture has its multitudes of whispered secrets that a small number of people are still able to pass on. It pleases me to think that, for example, there are only a few of Ruhlmann's workmen left and that only they can properly repair his ivory-inlaid furniture . . . and that I, because of luck and instinct, am one of the last to hold the secrets of haute couture.

Yet my final collection at Dior profoundly shocked the couture, though it was the first important definition of my style.

Motorcycle jackets in alligator, mink coats with sweater sleeves, turtleneck collars under finely cut flannel suits—those street inspirations all seemed very inelegant to a lot of people sitting on the gilt chairs of a couture salon. But this was the first collection in which I tried hard for poetic expression in my clothes. Social structures were

Saint Laurent with his longtime partner Pierre Bergé in the garden of their Paris apartment

breaking up. The street had a new pride, its own chic, and I found the street inspiring as I would often again. We must never confuse elegance with snobbery.

Yet again, anyone who reaches for great expression has to be careful of the ridiculous. Every art is delimited by its medium, mine by clothing. I used to say that what I do is a minor art. Maybe it is not so minor after all, but it is not fine art. I cannot pretend to do sculpture and make a woman the ridiculous pedestal of my pretensions. To render clothing poetic, yes—but one must preserve its dignity as clothing. I think of so many so-called avant-garde artists who push their material beyond its natural limits. They soil their own nests, destroy the forms that gave them space to work, and end up with chaotic junk. Yet when we do listen, we all can tell where the music ends and the noise begins.

So I am a classicist. I am fond of discipline. I find men's clothing fascinating because sometime between, say, 1930 and 1936 a handful of basic shapes were created and still prevail as a sort of scale of expression, with which every man can project his own

Saint Laurent at ease on a chair by Jean-Michel Frank, a favorite furniture designer personality and his own dignity. I've always wanted to give women the protection of that sort of basic wardrobe—protection from ridicule, freedom to be themselves. It pains me physically to see a woman victimized, rendered pathetic, by fashion.

I love women. I love all the bright and attractive people and things of this world, the flame and also the moth, the dancer and the dance. For the New Year, I send all my friends a poster that says simply "Love." I pass for a hypersensitive, reclusive neurotic, which I may well be, but I hope the year won't come when my anxieties and fatigue will destroy my love of this life, of all the things that inspire me—a line of music, a face in a Vermeer portrait, a character in an opera, or a model born in Harlem. I like to watch the way a model moves in my clothes, the way she gives them life, or if they are wrong, stillborn, the way her life rejects them. A good model can advance fashion by ten years.

Like Proust, I'm fascinated most of all by my perceptions of a world in awesome transition. That fascination is the fate of our age and it's also in my blood. In a square in Colmar, Frédéric Auguste Bartholdi, who designed the Statue of Liberty, set up his sculpture of the five continents. The model for America was my great-grandmother. She was a Mexican who fled to France when Maximilian's empire crumbled. And I can still see my mother and my sisters sitting in a little room in Paris with their suitcases after France lost Algeria. Like F. Scott Fitzgerald, I love a dying frenzy. I love Visconti. Decadence attracts me. It suggests a new world, and, for me, society's struggle between life and death is absolutely beautiful. In my own life, I've seen the last afterglow of the sumptuous Paris of before the war. The balls of the fifties—of Arturo Lopez, Charles de Beistegui—and the splendor of a vigorous haute couture. And then I knew the youthfulness of the sixties: Talitha and Paul Getty lying on a starlit terrace in Marrakesh, beautiful and damned, and a whole

Opposite:
Saint Laurent examines his sketches for his Ballets Russes collection, Fall/Winter, 1976–77. His faithful companion, Moujik, can be seen in the mirror.

Saint Laurent with Loulou de la Falaise, one of his chief assistants, draping fabrics and considering colors in his studio

generation assembled as if for eternity where the curtain of the past seemed to lift before an extraordinary future. And my heart has always been divided between the vestals of constancy and the avatars of change.

These are my impressions from Europe, and of a man who spends most of his time alone or hard at work. Of America I know very little, except that every time I visit I come away charged with

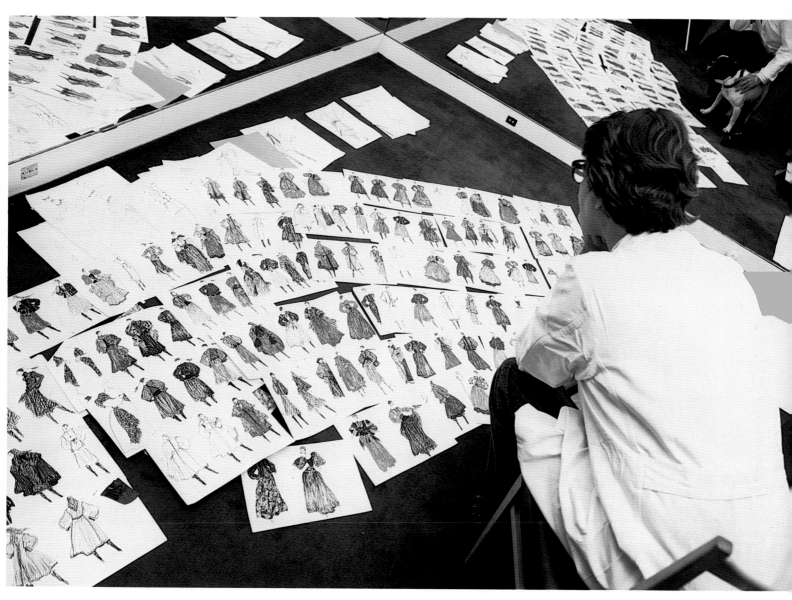

positive energy. I remember that when Pierre Bergé and I needed help to found the house of Yves Saint Laurent, to continue it, and finally to give it total independence, it was Americans who came forward and took risks defending my talent. And it is mainly thanks to the American press that my work was recognized, perhaps because America welcomes with open arms any original creation.

I have often said that I wish I had invented blue jeans: the most

Anne-Marie Muñoz, one of Saint Laurent's chief assistants

spectacular, the most practical, the most relaxed and nonchalant. They have expression, modesty, sex appeal, simplicity—all I hope for in my clothes.

Dressing is a way of life. It brings you joy. It can give you freedom and liberation, help you to find yourself and to move without restraint. Isn't elegance forgetting what one is wearing? What is wonderful about my art is that dream and reality can become one. There is just one step between the two.

Finding your own style is not easy, but once found it brings complete happiness. It gives you self-confidence, always.

After so many years of exploring, my art still fascinates me. I know of no greater exaltation. You think there is no going further, that everything is forever fixed and finished—and then, suddenly, depths and vistas reveal themselves that you thought out of reach and that your wealth of experience now fully opens to you. So many

Saint Laurent putting the finishing touches on an ensemble

Right: Saint Laurent at work in his studio

times did I believe myself impotent, broken, and desperate before the black curtain of weariness—and so many times did this curtain then rip itself apart to allow glimpses of limitless horizons, enabling me to feel my greatest joys, and, I dare to say, moments of true pride.

The great art, Prince Metternich said, is to last.

Yves Saint Laurent
(as told to G.Y. Dryansky)

Andy Warhol's portrait of Saint
Laurent, an oil painting dated 1972

An odalisque by Ingres

Proust

Daisy Fellowes

Concarneau

Picasso

Les Dames du Bois de Boulogne

Coco Chanel

Paul Claudel

Rudolph Nureyev

Diaghilev

Cocteau

A COLLAGE OF INSPIRATION

A Streetcar Named Desire

The retrospective exhibition of Yves Saint Laurent organized by The Metropolitan Museum of Art is not just a collection of clothes. For twenty-five years, Saint Laurent has fully exemplified Jean Cocteau's phrase: "In every landscape or still life, a painter always portrays himself."

For Yves—and herein lies his uniqueness—each collection is a means of bringing dreams to life, expressing fantasies, encountering myths, and creating out of them a contemporary fashion. Seeming to be nothing, a gown advances, and all at once the Duchesse de Guermantes appears. She turns and passes Natasha Rostov. In the distance, La Traviata faints into the arms of Germont *père*, while suddenly for Ludwig of Bavaria, alone in an empty theater, Wagner sounds an English horn. Beyond the mists of Neuschwanstein, Elisabeth of Austria bridles her horse. Already she is costumed by Christian Bérard and talks like Jean Cocteau. A verse of Apollinaire gleams like a motto on a standard. The veiled women of Morocco throw Marlene Dietrich into Gary Cooper's arms. Marlon Brando's blue jeans flash past as he alights from his streetcar. Zizi

Louis Jouvet

Paley and de Noailles

Maxim's (by Sem)

Jean-Michel Frank

Zizi Jeanmaire

Les Yeux d'Elsa by Claus Ohm

Senso by Visconti

Madeleine Renaud and Jean-Louis Barrault

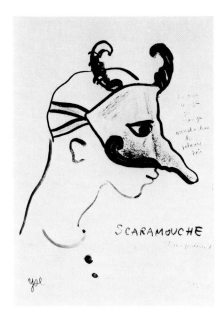

La Théâtre de l'Athénée

Mayakovski and Lili Brik

Les Enfants du Paradis

Kyoto

Christian Bérard

Goya

Wagner

King Ludwig of Bavaria

Madeleine Vionnet

Jeanmaire winds her feather boa around Goya's Maja. Scarlett O'Hara borrows Rhett Butler's hat. Yet again Callas advances to stab Scarpia, while Matisse and Andy Warhol boogie-woogie with Mondrian.

Here comes Visconti leading the procession: Chanel leans on Diaghilev's shoulder—Nureyev steps forward between Lili Brik and Tatiana Liberman. The Ladies of the Bois de Boulogne button up their raincoats in front of Maria Casarès, while Arletty contemplates Jean-Louis Barrault in the mirror of the children of paradise. Madeleine Renaud lies half buried in Beckett's sand. Christian Dior.

Elisabeth of Austria

New York City

Vivaldi

drapes Madeleine Vionnet's bias cut, and Daisy Fellowes, a shoe perched on her forehead, is overpowered by Schiaparelli.

One gown follows another. Those designed for late suppers at Maxim's mingle with ensembles for the Brasserie Lipp. Sailors in peajackets set off for Deauville. Seated on Eileen Gray chairs beneath a Picasso hung by Jean-Michel Frank, Marie Laure de Noailles and Nathalie Paley watch the spectacle.

A bare shoulder emerges and here is a Rubens from the Munich Alte Pinakothek. Abruptly the music changes, and the Turkish bath of Ingres materializes. At last, here comes the bride. She arrives from the Prado and leads Velázquez by the hand. Applause crackles like gunfire. Yves has supervised everything, seen everything, listened to everything. He comes forward, his mind reeling from all these dreams that have collided. Pale, spent, happy.

And meanwhile, in the Majorelle gardens of Marrakesh, the palm trees sway in the breeze blowing from the Atlas Mountains.

Pierre Bergé

Velázquez

30

Christian Dior

Eileen Gray

Elsa Schiaparelli

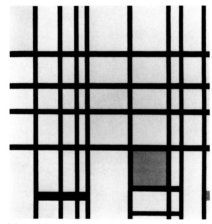

Mondrian

Deauville

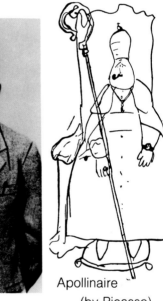

Samuel Beckett

Apollinaire
(by Picasso)

Maria Callas

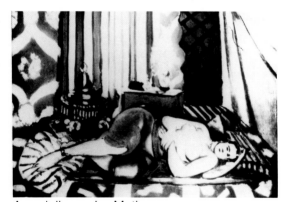

An odalisque by Matisse

Marlene Dietrich

Verdi

YVES SAINT LAURENT

Paloma Picasso (by Cecil Beaton)

What is happening to you? This morning you looked like a charming youth dreaming of Eton, with your little *canotier*.* I met you for lunch at Kaspia and you were a naughty baboushka with a definite taste for caviar and vodka. Was it you that almost got run over by a bus on the Place de la Concorde or was it in fact a real matador fighting off the traffic in his bullfighter's costume? I know, you have been going through my closets, you have been playing around with my Saint Laurents. Well, now, make up your mind, it's either red satin or lamé, and hurry up or we'll be late for the opera. Let's enjoy the thrill of a total Saint Laurent immersion.

*straw boater

Yves is marvelous about bringing out all the facets in you. He offers you the chance to play up to the clothes without feeling self-conscious about them. His fashion doesn't tamper with your personality, it promotes it. He's classic and he's aclassic and it's up to you to tilt the balance one way or the other.

It's hard to separate Yves from Yves' work. I doubt if he can himself. I can't believe he wants to. Yves is very passionate; he loves quality, he craves beauty, he demands and commands them. He is absolutist in his friendship as in his passions; he is shy but doesn't hold anything back. How to describe an admiration that has never been disappointed: I could trace my life through his collections.

Paloma Picasso-Lopez

Marella Agnelli (by Richard Avedon)

One cannot speak of style without thinking of Yves Saint Laurent. Style is an indefinable, mysterious element that permeates every visual moment of our lives, an elusive quality that evolves and changes, comes to torment us, and then leaves, returning to haunt those of us who remain constant to its essence in spite of its fickle nature. Out of the designer's imagination and intuition, via the staff that helps him to master the technical and commercial aspects of production, style evolves from dreams, desires, and hopes to become fashion. Contemporary style—that is, the fashion of these last twenty years—can be likened to a huge, multicolored kite kept afloat by an increasingly turbulent wind, a kite whose strings have been kept in turn miraculously taut or slack in the controlling hands of Yves Saint Laurent. Launched into the wind by Yves in the early sixties, that multicolored kite soared into the sky and is still flying today.

To Saint Laurent goes the credit for creating the look (or should we say the essence) of our times, and also for being one of the first, if not the very first, to reproduce that look, like a work of art, in order to make it accessible to a wider public. Through Saint Laurent's Rive Gauche _prêt-à-porter_ line, fashion took a big step into the future, leaving behind the remote, elitist character it had had in the past.

There are many factors that have helped to keep this magic kite flying. In addition to Yves' genius, there have been the inspiration of Loulou de la Falaise, the invaluable collaboration of Anne Marie Muñoz, the imaginative search for materials by Gustav Zumsteg, the constant guidance of Pierre Bergé, and much, much more. But, most important, there is the wind—the strong wind of talent, of change, of poetry, of chance . . . all of the different names by which elegance is known.

Marella Agnelli

When you put something on from Yves Saint Laurent's couture, there is an immediate sensual experience: everything, no matter what it's made of, is always lined in silk satin. That detail is emblematic of his total attitude toward women. He wants to spoil them, to envelop them in the pleasure of his clothes. He is also very protective.

Saint Laurent designs for women with double lives. His day clothes help a woman confront the world of strangers. They permit her to go everywhere without drawing unwelcome attention, and with their somewhat masculine quality, they give her a certain force, prepare her for encounters that may become a conflict of wills. In the evening, when a woman chooses to be with those she is fond of, he makes her seductive.

Behind this impulse to serve a modern woman, to accommodate her life, there is a modesty which is all the more apparent when Yves Saint Laurent designs for the cinema. Some designers make sure their clothes are always identifiable when they do clothes for a film. Saint Laurent carefully reads the script, and with his clothes

Catherine Deneuve (in François Truffaut's film *La Sirène du Mississippi*)

he creates an important expression of the role and even of the scene. He has designed film costumes for me ever since Luis Buñuel's *Belle de Jour* in 1966. When you act in cinema, you are not constantly in the role, as with the theater. You spend a long time getting ready for a few minutes on camera, and then you have to be there, right in the role. When I'm dressed by Saint Laurent, I have that extra protection of being able to step into the role when I put on my costume. It is already so much the personage, the someone else an actress has to be able to be.

In *Belle de Jour*, there is a scene in which my dress is torn off my body. Saint Laurent designed a jersey dress, but underneath, without any prompting, he put strips of Velcro. When the dress was torn, the sound the Velcro made was already the expression of a rape. That is what he is all about: expression. Some designers do clothing that is merely color and shape; his always says something.

Catherine Deneuve

1936 August 1. Yves Mathieu Saint Laurent born in Oran, Algeria, to Charles and Lucienne (Wilbaux) Mathieu Saint Laurent.

1947 At age eleven, Yves sees a production of Molière's *Ecole des Femmes* directed by Louis Jouvet and is so impressed by the sets and costumes designed by Christian Bérard that he recreates a miniature version at home to amuse his parents and two sisters.

new to Paris, new to France, of the rising current of youth taking over." (U.S. *Vogue*, March 1958)

Marie-Louise Bousquet, French representative of *Harper's Bazaar*, introduces Yves to Pierre Bergé.

Saint Laurent's second collection for Dior, in which he drastically lowers hemlines to sixteen inches above the floor, opens on July 31. "The revealing of the bosom was Paris's most exciting new ges-

Tricot

Crocodile
with
mink
1960

YVES SAINT LAURENT

1953 Yves wins first prize in a competition sponsored by the International Wool Secretariat for a black cocktail dress.

1955 He completes his formal studies in Oran and goes to Paris.

Yves attends a professional cutting school for three months. In June, Michel de Brunhoff, editor of French *Vogue*, sees his drawings and is struck by their similarity to the "A-line" designs in Christian Dior's forthcoming Fall/Winter Collection. Before the collection is presented, de Brunhoff introduces Yves to Dior, who hires him immediately as an assistant.

1957 October. Christian Dior dies suddenly of a stroke.

November 15. Yves Saint Laurent is named head designer of the house of Dior.

1958 January 30. Saint Laurent introduces his first collection at Dior, featuring the "trapeze" look. After the showing, Parisians demonstrate in the streets, chanting his name and proclaiming that Yves Saint Laurent has saved France. Since the house of Dior is responsible for nearly 50 percent of French fashion exports at this time, Saint Laurent's success is deemed crucial for the French economy. "All over Paris there is the sensation,

ture, particularly at Dior, where the raised waistline and shallow bodice emphasized the décolletage." (*Harper's Bazaar*, September 1958)

1959 Saint Laurent creates costumes for Roland Petit's ballet *Cyrano de Bergerac*.

In his fall collection, Saint Laurent at Dior "raises the skirt to the knees, belts every waist, and pulls in the skirt to a tight knee-band. The confidence invested in him last year is swept away by the outcry of the press, directed mainly at the skirt." (Georgina Howell, *In Vogue*, Thames and Hudson, 1976)

1960 Saint Laurent's Spring/Summer Collection is highly praised as one of the most beautiful and youthful the house has ever produced.

The controversial Fall/Winter Collection features knit turtlenecks and black leather jackets. "The beat look is the news at Dior . . . pale zombie faces; leather suits and coats; knitted caps and high turtleneck collars, black endlessly." (British *Vogue*, 1960)

September. Yves Saint Laurent is drafted by the French Army but is soon hospitalized with a nervous collapse.

October. Marc Bohan is named head designer at Dior, replacing Saint Laurent, who is discharged from the Army in November and enters a private clinic for convalescence.

1961 May. Saint Laurent sues the house of Dior because of their refusal to reinstate him and wins a share of the profits for the period during which he designed.

September. Saint Laurent announces plans to open his own couture house in partnership with Pierre Bergé, with backing from J. Mack Robinson of Atlanta, Georgia.

A CHRONOLOGY

Saint Laurent designs sets and costumes for Roland Petit's ballet *Les Forains* for French television and the sets and costumes for "Spectacle Zizi Jeanmaire" at the Théâtre de l'Alhambra.

December. The first dress to appear under the Saint Laurent label is designed for Mrs. Arturo Lopez-Willshaw.

1962 January 29. Saint Laurent presents his first collection under his own name at a rented mansion on the rue Spontini. *Life* magazine calls his designs "the best suits since Chanel."

Saint Laurent's Fall/Winter Collection features the peajacket and the Norman smock. "In 1962 I put a simple peacoat in couture. I was saying it's OK to wear it. The ones with money bought it from me. The ones without money bought it from the flea market." (Yves Saint Laurent, 1977)

"Saint Laurent's second collection from his own house was a glittering *tour de force*, greeted with the special kind of emotional fervour reserved for such occasions." (U.S. *Vogue*, September 1962)

Saint Laurent designs sets and costumes for two more Roland Petit ballets, *Les Chants de Maldoror* and *Rhapsodie Espagnole*.

1963 Diana Vreeland heralds the Spring/Summer Collection: "At Saint Laurent, the room was a blaze of yellow forsythia standing tree-high. The clothes beautiful and touching with not a hard line anywhere; you feel the charm of his approach to fashion the moment you enter the house." (U.S. *Vogue*, March 1963)

Saint Laurent designs the sets and costumes for "Spectacle Zizi Jeanmaire" at the Théâtre National Populaire.

1964 The Fall/Winter Collection earns international admiration: "At Saint Laurent everything is fluid; no hard lines, no sharp stops or starts; enchanting tunic ideas; high small armholes and long discreet appealing suits; langorous evening dresses." (Diana Vreeland, U.S. *Vogue*, September 1964)

August 3. John Fairchild, publisher of *Women's Wear Daily*, writes in his diary: "Yves Saint Laurent—his collection named "Une Femme." Saint Laurent's ode to the tunic and the tiered dress, inspired, as he said, by the Eighth Wonder, Chanel. The most beautiful collection I had ever seen in Paris, marking the return to gracious, beautiful, refined clothes. A complete reaction against tough chic. WWD opinion, strongly for—the rest of the fashion world, against."

Saint Laurent designs the costumes for *Le Mariage de Figaro* and *Il Faut Passer par les Nuages* for the company of Madeleine Renaud and Jean-Louis Barrault at the Odéon Théâtre de France.

1965 Diana Vreeland pronounces the Spring/Summer Collection: "completely dressmaking. Great subtlety and finish. French, pretty, and very feminine." (U.S. *Vogue*, April 1965)

The Fall/Winter collection features the "Mondrian" dresses, "the dress of tomorrow—the assertive abstraction, a semaphore flag, sharply defined in crisp white jersey, perfectly proportioned to flatter your figure." (*Harper's Bazaar*, September 1965)

Saint Laurent designs costumes for two Roland Petit ballets, *Adage et Variations* and *Notre Dame de Paris*. He also designs costumes for Marguerite Duras' *Des Journées entières dans les Arbres* for the company of Madeleine Renaud and Jean-Louis Barrault.

1966 The Spring/Summer Collection includes a navy coatdress and a peacoat. "Saint Laurent has gone to sea in a spaceship. Join his navy and see the world!" exclaimed *Harper's Bazaar* (April 1966).

The Fall/Winter Collection features Saint Laurent's first "smoking" for women and his first "Pop art" dresses. "Saint Laurent's autumn collection includes a few jokes, chiefly the pop art dresses inspired by Andy Warhol." (Georgina Howell, *In Vogue*)

September 26. The first Saint Laurent Rive Gauche boutique is opened at 21, rue de Tournon, Paris. "Certainly it would be impossible to copy the couture designs in ready-to-wear. No matter how much I might want to at times, the handwork could not be duplicated by machines. For that reason, I conceive of the *prêt-à-porter* designs differently, in terms of machine fabrication." (Yves Saint Laurent, October 1978)

Saint Laurent designs the wardrobe for Arletty in Jean Cocteau's *Les Monstres Sacrés* at the Théâtre des Ambassadeurs, Paris.

1967 The Spring/Summer Collection features Saint Laurent's "African" dresses, "a fantasy of primitive genius—shells and jungle jewelry clustered to cover the bosom and hips, latticed to bare the midriff." (*Harper's Bazaar*, March 1967)

Saint Laurent designs costumes for Edward Albee's *A Deli-*

cate Balance for the company of Madeleine Renaud and Jean-Louis Barrault. He also designs the wardrobe for Catherine Deneuve in Luis Buñuel's film Belle de Jour.

J. Mack Robinson sells his interest in Yves Saint Laurent to Charles of the Ritz, later Lanvin-Charles of the Ritz, owned by the American Richard Salomon.

Editions Tchou publishes Yves Saint Laurent's illustrated book La Vilaine Lulu.

1968 The Spring/Summer Collection features the safari look, see-through dresses, and "the shirt-dress the world has been waiting for." (U.S. Vogue, March 1968)

Saint Laurent designs costumes for "Spectacle Zizi Jeanmaire" at the Olympia and the wardrobe for Catherine Deneuve in Alain Cavalier's film La Chamade.

1969 The Spring/Summer Collection includes beaded mini-dresses for evening. "Marvellously decorative vivid gypsies." (U.S. Vogue, March 1969)

The Fall/Winter Collection is highlighted by a black-and-white patchwork fur coat; U.S. Vogue proclaims 1969 the year of Saint Laurent's "divine coats."

Saint Laurent designs the wardrobe for Catherine Deneuve in François Truffaut's film La Sirène du Mississippi.

1970 The Spring/Summer Collection features "coats so eclectic that they know no low of the day.... Yves Saint Laurent patterns the seventies to perfection." (Harper's Bazaar, March 1970)

The Fall/Winter Collection includes "ravishingly romantic silk shawls in documentary prints... Yves Saint Laurent glorifies the night with a soft stroke." (Harper's Bazaar, September 1970)

Saint Laurent designs costumes for "Revue Zizi Jeanmaire" at the Casino de Paris and for "Spectacle Sylvie Vartan" at the Olympia.

1971 The Spring/Summer Collection features the "forties" look and the blazer. "The collection of [Spring 1971] that everyone calls 'kitsch' (I hate that word), that was a reaction against the turn fashion had taken ...the gypsies, all those long skirts and bangles...so I did my collection as a kind of humorous protest, only everyone took it seriously. Then I became more sure of myself when I returned to my true style." (Yves Saint Laurent, 1972)

The Fall/Winter Collection "can be visualized on a certain kind of woman. She has style, adventurousness. And what she's going to want first is his new smocking coat—his only coat shape—and the most prophetic in Paris.... And the most talked-about dresses: the rustle of taffeta he called Proust dresses. The coquetry of these!—the swish of big taffeta skirts—they are going to bring taffeta into our lives...." (U.S. Vogue, September 1971)

Saint Laurent designs sets and costumes for "Spectacle Johnny Hallyday" at the Palais des Sports.

Richard Salomon sells Lanvin-Charles of the Ritz to the Squibb pharmaceutical company and becomes chancellor of Brown University, enabling Saint Laurent to become independent.

1972 "The fashion hit this wonderful, European spring was the collection of Yves Saint Laurent.... The man is, pure and simple, the greatest fashion designer in the world today. Saint Laurent, still in his early thirties, this season showed the best collection he's done in several years." (James Brady, Harper's Bazaar, March 1972)

At the Fall/Winter Collection, "the buyers brought Yves out to take three encores.... He's still tops and is today's Chanel," according to James Brady reporting in Harper's Bazaar (September 1972). Nina Hyde of The Washington Post announces that Saint Laurent "has

changed the face—and perhaps the future—of fashion." (November 1972)

Saint Laurent designs costumes for "Revue Zizi Jeanmaire" at the Casino de Paris and the costumes for "Spectacle Sylvie Vartan" at the Olympia.

1973 The Spring/Summer Collection features "the fluid, body-conscious chemise—ankle-length—sensational new look for evening." (U.S. Vogue, March 1973)

With the Fall/Winter Collection, "Saint Laurent leads the way," according to U.S. Vogue, September 1973. "His key looks just happen to be the key looks—the best example of everything modern, upbeat, and attractive in every category of dressing for every minute of the day. Not that his basic formula has changed...this year he has simply taken it to its highest level. It is Couture at its healthiest: a way for real women to look whenever, wherever—it is perfection!"

Saint Laurent designs the costumes for Maia Plissetskaia in Roland Petit's ballet La Rose Malade, for Colin Higgins' Harold and Maude produced by Madeleine Renaud and Jean-Louis Barrault, for Jeanne Moreau, Delphine Seyrig, and Gérard Depardieu in Peter Handke's La Chevauchée sur le lac de Constance, and for Roland Petit's ballet Schéhérézade.

1974 Saint Laurent designs the wardrobe for Anny Duperey in Alain Resnais' film Stavisky.

The Galerie Proscénium in Paris exhibits models of Saint Laurent's theatrical costumes and set designs.

July. The couture house is moved to 5, avenue Marceau.

1975 The Spring/Summer Collection features a "little dress, narrow and neat and quick to move in—it's why everyone is going to want to be in a dress again!" and "for the women who love pants, the most sensational pants look in Paris" (U.S. *Vogue*, March 1975)

The Fall/Winter Collection prompts a long feature article in the September issue of U.S. *Vogue*: "Nobody understands better than Saint Laurent that evening is many different moods of dressing—there isn't one he hasn't thought out and thought through...and done something beautiful about. Something that doesn't exist anywhere else—such as his new 'restaurant dresses'...."

1976 The Spring/Summer Collection features the Ballets Russes dresses, and his Fall/Winter Collection creates an international sensation, being featured on the front page of *The New York Times* as a "revolutionary" collection "that will change the course of fashion around the world." "[This] collection will be colorful, lively, bright. The fabrics will be woven like in Morocco, striped, like djellabahs, in wool. This collection will be the continuation of the last. I had so much to say last time I couldn't say it all. This time I'll say the rest. I don't know if this is my best collection. But it is my most beautiful collection." (Yves Saint Laurent, 1976)

"What Yves Saint Laurent has done, with his latest collection, is to remind us that fashion, in its radical form of haute couture, *is* costume ....It strikingly illustrates the degree of sophistication attained by fashion's analysis of history....It's not nostalgia for the past, but for the eternal present which lies on the other side of the past." (Pierre Schneider, U.S. *Vogue*, September 1976)

1977 The Spring/Summer Collection prompts U.S. *Vogue* to report: "What [YSL] does tends to give designers the courage to do their own thing. *His* own thing is very simple: sexiness, gaiety...deliciousness!"

The Fall/Winter Collection featuring the Chinese designs is proclaimed by French *Vogue* in September as "a superb collection."

"The changing world of evening ...and the feeling for unstoppered splendour and luxe that reached its most seductive heights in the ravishing chinoiseries of Saint Laurent." (U.S. *Vogue*, October 1977)

"It was a deeply egocentric show! I returned to an age of elegance and wealth. In many ways I returned to my own past. I put into the collection all my favourite painters and operas. It was theatre! It was also what is still hidden inside me. I grew up in a generation and a world of elegance. Tradition still flickered! And yet at the same time, I wanted to transform it. One is caught between the past holding you, and the future pushing you. It's why I am split in two. And I always will be. Because I knew one world and felt the other." (Yves Saint Laurent, 1977)

1978 Saint Laurent designs costumes and sets for Jean Cocteau's *L'Aigle a deux têtes* at the Théâtre de l'Athénée–Louis Jouvet. He also designs the costume for Ingrid Caven's recital at Le Pigall's.

The Galerie Proscenium, Paris, mounts a second exhibition of his theatrical costumes and set designs.

The Fall/Winter Collection "is very elegant, very provocative and very modern—which perhaps seems contradictory. At the same time I wanted something very pure, I introduced into this purity certain unexpected things: sharp collars, little hats, tasseled shoes. I wanted to give haute couture a kind of wink, a sense of humor—to replace street gags with a more suitable wit, to introduce the whole sense of freedom one sees in the street into high fashion—to give couture the same provocative and arrogant look as punk—but, of course, with luxury and dignity, and style." (Yves Saint Laurent, 1978)

1979 The Spring/Summer Collection: "I was completely obsessed with this collection. All my life is ex-

pressed in it. I wanted everyone to understand that my concept of clothes is timeless. And it has taken me twenty years to prove it." (Yves Saint Laurent, 1982)

The Fall/Winter Collection features his "Picasso" designs.

1980 The Spring/Summer Collection "reconfirms the dynamic effect of Yves Saint Laurent on how women dress—a wonderful force for over two decades." (U.S. *Vogue*, January 1980)

Saint Laurent designs the costumes and sets for *Cher Menteur*, a play by Jerome Kilty adapted by Jean Cocteau, presented at the Théâtre de l'Athénée–Louis Jouvet with Edwige Feuillière and Jean Marais.

1981 Saint Laurent designs a costume for Marguerite Yourcenar's induction into the Académie Française.

1982 Yves Saint Laurent celebrates the 20th anniversary of the house of Saint Laurent.

YVES SAINT LAURENT
BY DUANE MICHALS

1. Theatrical cape of ostrich feathers made for Zizi Jean-maire in 1970. No. 89

2. Velvet dress with taffeta ruffles from the Fall/Winter Collection 1977–78. No. 133

2

3. Lace evening dress with chiffon-and-marabou jacket from the Spring/Summer Collection 1980. No. 161

4. Detail of colorplate 3

3

5. Evening dress of printed chiffon from the Fall/Winter Collection 1977–78. No. 134

6. Lace-backed cocktail dress of black crepe from the Fall/Winter Collection 1970–71. No. 94

7. "Matisse" evening dress of taffeta from the Fall/Winter Collection 1981–82. No. 190

5

6

9

8. Evening dress of gold-threaded silk organdy from the Spring/ Summer Collection 1981. No. 179

9. Cashmere coat from the Fall/ Winter Collection 1980–81. No. 167

10. Two-piece evening dress of velvet and crepe from the Fall/ Winter Collection 1982–83. No. 202

10

11

11. Four "African" dresses from
the Spring/Summer Collection
1967. Nos. 54–57

12. Detail of colorplate 11

14

13. Detail of colorplate 14

14. Three evening ensembles from the Spring/Summer Collection 1977. Nos. 121–23

15. Wedding dress of ottoman and satin patchwork commissioned by H.R.H. Madame la Duchesse d'Orléans in August 1969. No. 79

15

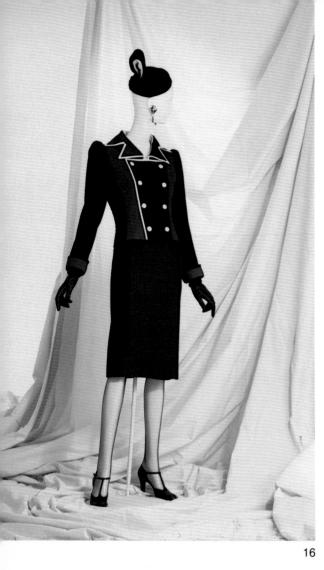

16. "Picasso" suit from the Fall/Winter Collection 1979–80. No. 150

17. Wool suit from the Fall/Winter Collection 1982–83. No. 203

18. Satin tunic and velvet skirt from the Fall/Winter Collection 1962–63. No. 23

16

17

20

20. "Russian" evening ensemble of hand-decorated gold lamé and jet trimmed with mink from the Fall/Winter Collection 1976–77. No. 116

21. Detail of colorplate 20

22. Bejeweled jacket from the Fall/ Winter Collection 1979–80. No. 151

22

23. Wool pantsuit and crepe de chine blouse from the Spring/Summer Collection 1978. No. 135

24. Three-piece day ensemble from the Spring/Summer Collection 1982. No. 194

25. Wool peajacket and shantung pants from the Spring/Summer Collection 1962. No. 21

24

23

26. Five "Chinese" ensembles from the Fall/Winter Collection 1977–78. Nos. 128–32

27. Taffeta cocktail dresses from the Fall/Winter Collection 1981–82. Nos. 188 and 189

28. Fox mini-coat from the Spring/Summer Collection 1971. No. 98

29. Four-piece day ensemble from the Fall/Winter Collection 1979–80. No. 154

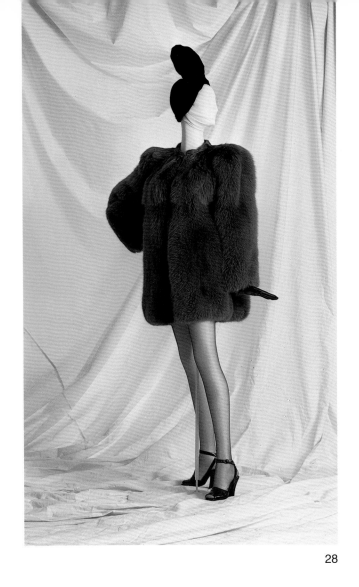

28

29

30. "Spanish" day ensemble from the Spring/Summer Collection 1977. No. 120

31. Mini-dress with gold embroidered snake from the Fall/Winter Collection 1966–67. No. 52

32. Beaded jacket from 1983 worn with mousseline blouse and gray flannel pants to represent the look of 1973. No. 213

31

30

33. Detail of colorplate 34

34. Appliquéd "Picasso" evening dress from the Fall/Winter Collection 1979—80. No. 155

34

35. Wool suit with satin blouse from the Fall/Winter Collection 1981–82. No. 187

36. Cocktail suit of ottoman and wool with organdy blouse from the Spring/Summer Collection 1981. No. 178

37. Detail of colorplate 36

36

35

38. "Toreador" ensemble of gold lamé and black velvet from the Fall/Winter Collection 1979–80. No. 153

39. "Shakespeare" wedding dress of brocade and damask from the Fall/Winter Collection 1980–81. No. 170

38

39

42

40. Wool dress with organdy collar from the Spring/Summer Collection 1963. No. 27

41. Day dress of gabardine and piqué from the Spring/Summer Collection 1963. No. 195

42. Four-piece plaid day ensemble from the Fall/Winter Collection 1982. No. 166

41

43

43. Crepe day dress from the Spring/Summer Collection 1962. No. 22

44. Beaded evening dresses from the Spring/Summer Collection 1969. Nos. 77 and 78

45. Sequined evening coat from the Fall/Winter Collection 1964–65. No. 35

44

46. Four "African" dresses from the Spring/Summer Collection 1967. Nos. 58–61

47. "Safari" jacket from July 1968. No. 70

48. Detail of colorplate 46

49. "Picasso" dress of black satin decorated with sequins from the Fall/Winter Collection 1979–80. No. 152

50. "Shakespeare" evening suit of velvet from the Fall/Winter Collection 1980–81. No. 168

51. Detail of colorplate 50

52

52. "Pop art" dresses of wool jersey from the Fall/Winter Collection 1966–67. Nos. 50 and 51

53. Suede patchwork coats from the Fall/Winter Collection 1970–71. Nos. 95 and 96

54. Satin evening jacket embroidered with a line from Cocteau from the Fall/Winter Collection 1980–81. No. 169

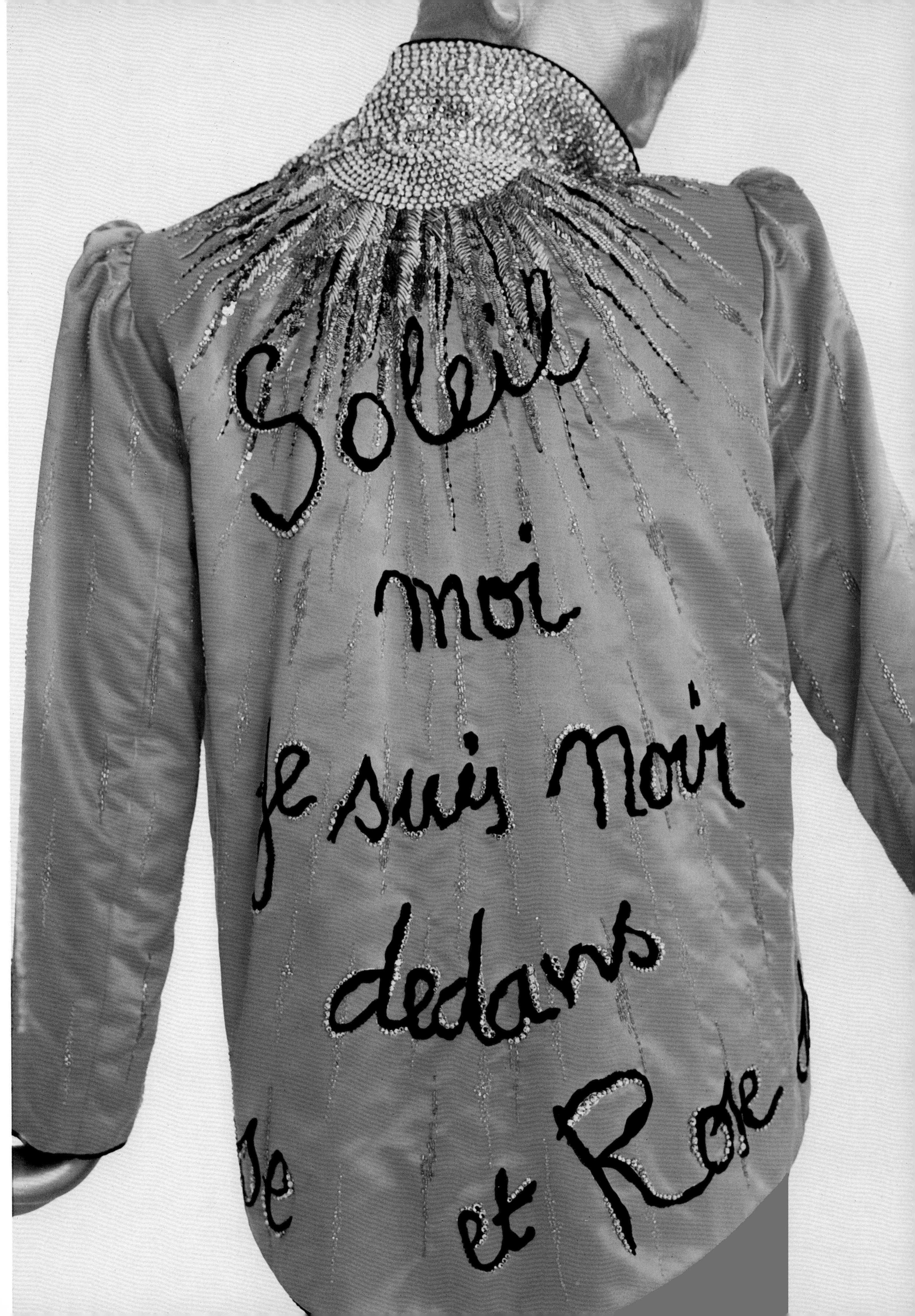
Soleil
moi
Je suis Noir
dedans
et Rose

55. "Mondrian" dresses of wool jersey from the Fall/Winter Collection 1965–66. Nos. 42 and 43

57

58

56. Detail of colorplate 57

57. "African" dresses from the Spring/Summer Collection 1967. Nos. 62–64

58. Detail of colorplate 57

59

60

59. Crepe georgette evening dresses worn with gold body sculpture from the Fall/Winter Collection 1969–70. Nos. 86 and 87

60. Detail of colorplate 59

AN ILLUSTRATED SURVEY

Yves Saint Laurent's first dress for
Dior, photographed by Richard
Avedon in 1955 for *Harper's Bazaar*

2

The entries that follow describe in chronological order all of the couture designs by Yves Saint Laurent illustrated in this book. The dates given refer to the seasonal collections for which each model was made. The first fifteen descriptions are for designs done by Yves Saint Laurent after he assumed the artistic direction of the couture house of Christian Dior. The rest of the entries are for the designs produced under Yves Saint Laurent's own label. All of the costumes, unless otherwise noted, are in the collection of Yves Saint Laurent. For the most part the accessories shown with the costumes were reproduced by Yves Saint Laurent to represent those used with the models at the original couture showings.

1. DAY DRESS of coral linen in "trapeze" style. Christian Dior Spring/Summer Collection 1958, designed by YSL
The Metropolitan Museum of Art
Gift of Bernice Chrysler Garbisch, 1977
(1977.108.1)

2. COAT DRESS of gray wool bouclé in "trapeze" style. Christian Dior Spring/Summer Collection 1958, designed by YSL
The Metropolitan Museum of Art
Gift of Imogene Schubert,
1958 (CI 58.66ab)

3. EVENING DRESS of white net embroidered with silver thread, sequins, and rhinestones in "Trapeze" style. Christian Dior Spring/Summer Collection 1958, designed by YSL
The Metropolitan Museum of Art
Gift of Edgar Willian and Bernice Chrysler Garbisch, 1977 (1977.329.5)

3

Audrey Hepburn wearing a Saint
Laurent dress at Maxim's,
photographed by Richard Avedon
for *Harper's Bazaar* (September
1959); with her are Art Buchwald
and two other models wearing
gowns by Pierre Balmain and Jean
Patou

4. EVENING DRESS of lavender
   velvet in "trapeze" style. Christian Dior Fall/Winter Collection
   1958–59, designed by YSL
   The Metropolitan Museum of Art
   Gift of Baron Philippe de Rothschild,
   1983

5. DAY DRESS with matching
   jacket and wide belt of green
   wool tweed. Christian Dior Fall/
   Winter Collection 1958–59,
   designed by YSL
   The Metropolitan Museum of Art
   Gift of Mrs. John Chambers Hughes,
   1960 (CI 60.44.2abc)

5

4

"Once we needed to have changes in fashion. New looks and new disguises. But now it is ridiculous to think that clothes must change, that hemlines must change, that women want pants this season and not the next. Everything in fashion is settled. Women will change their clothes, but always within the ideas that we have now developed." *Yves Saint Laurent, 1972*

6. COCKTAIL DRESS with matching belt of red silk faille. Christian Dior Fall/Winter Collection
1959–60, designed by YSL
The Metropolitan Museum of Art
Gift of Joyce von Bothmer,
1976 (1976.117.5ab)

7. COCKTAIL DRESS of gunme-
tal-gray silk taffeta. Christian
Dior Fall/Winter Collection
1959–60, designed by YSL
The Metropolitan Museum of Art
Gift of Joyce von Bothmer,
1976 (1976.117.3)

8. COCKTAIL DRESS of black and
white wool and mohair. Christian Dior Fall/Winter Collection
1959–60, designed by YSL
Lent by Edward C. Blum Laboratory of
Fashion Institute of Technology

7

8

"One of the problems with fashion today is there are fewer and fewer designers in the old manner who understand how to cut. It's perfection of line. It's perfection of material. It's how to work with a beautiful fabric, to give life to a wonderful material. To tame it by keeping it alive." *Yves Saint Laurent, 1982*

9

9. COCKTAIL DRESS of black crepe with asymmetrical neckline. Christian Dior Fall/Winter Collection 1959–60, designed by YSL
Lent by Victoire Doutreleau to Yves Saint Laurent

10. COCKTAIL DRESS of black chiffon trimmed with black velvet ribbon bands. Christian Dior Fall/Winter Collection 1959–60, designed by YSL
Lent by Victoire Doutreleau to Yves Saint Laurent

11. JACKET of black wool and satin ribbon trimmed with black mink. Christian Dior Fall/Winter Collection 1959–60, designed by YSL
Lent by Victoire Doutreleau to Yves Saint Laurent

10

12. DRESS with matching jacket and contour belt of black silk faille and long scarf of black satin. Christian Dior Fall/Winter Collection, 1959–60, designed by YSL
The Metropolitan Museum of Art
Gift of Mrs. John Chambers Hughes, 1961 (CI 61.19a–d)

13. EVENING DRESS of pale green silk shantung in a "coat dress" style. Christian Dior Spring/Summer Collection 1960, designed by YSL
The Metropolitan Museum of Art
Gift of Baron Philippe de Rothschild, 1983

14. EVENING ENSEMBLE with overblouse of black nylon net trimmed in jet beads and skirt of ivory silk faille. Christian Dior Fall/Winter Collection 1960–61, designed by YSL
The Metropolitan Museum of Art
Gift of Mrs. Charles B. Wrightsman, 1962 (CI 62.50.5ab)

13

14

Saint Laurent's crocodile jacket with a mink collar as it appeared in *Vogue* (October 1960) photographed by Irving Penn

15. DAY ENSEMBLE with coat of gray wool fleece shown with two-piece dress of dark blue wool. Christian Dior Fall/Winter Collection 1960–61, designed by YSL

The Metropolitan Museum of Art
Coat: Gift of Mrs. Henry Rogers Benjamin, 1965 (CI 65.14.23);
dress: Gift of Kay Kerr Uebel, 1974 (1974.386.16ab)

"If my clothes are right, and I believe they are, it is because I think I understand what women want. I am interested in absolutely everything in life today. I want to see everything, read everything. Go to films. Read newspapers." *Yves Saint Laurent, 1972*

101

16. EVENING DRESS of black embossed silk crepe georgette with jet-embroidered bodice; shown with headdress of black velvet and taffeta flowers and shoes of black crepe. Created for Mrs. Arturo Lopez-Willshaw in 1961, this is the first dress designed by YSL in his own couture house and bears his label with the model number 00001.
Gift of Mrs. Arturo Lopez-Willshaw to Yves Saint Laurent

17. EVENING OVERBLOUSE of black silk chiffon covered with shaped silk leaves and trimmed with black satin ribbon; shown with white silk skirt. Spring/Summer Collection 1962
The Metropolitan Museum of Art
Gift of Lee Radziwill, 1977
(1977.157.12)

18. DRESS of red and pink embossed silk. Created for Victoire Doutreleau in 1961
Lent by Victoire Doutreleau to Yves Saint Laurent

17

18

19. EVENING DRESS of black cotton piqué with skirt embroidered in floral pattern in red, pink, and orange. Spring/Summer Collection 1962
Gift of the Vicomtesse de Ribes to Yves Saint Laurent

1962

Pea jacket
gold buttons

white shantung
pants

Navy leather
sandal

20. SUIT of natural silk shantung, shown with cowboy hat of natural linen and shoes of beige leather. Spring/Summer Collection 1962
Lent by Victoire Doutreleau to Yves Saint Laurent

21. DAY ENSEMBLE with pea-jacket of navy-blue wool, pants and sleeveless blouse of white silk shantung. Spring/Summer Collection 1962
(Colorplate 25)

22. DAY DRESS of beige silk crepe with double-tiered pleated skirt; shown with black straw hat and black leather shoes. Spring/Summer Collection 1962
Lent by Mme Christian de Merindol to Yves Saint Laurent
(Colorplate 43)

23. COCKTAIL ENSEMBLE with tunic of pearl-gray satin and skirt of gray velvet; shown with gray velvet hat and black suede shoes. Fall/Winter Collection 1962–63
(Colorplate 18)

"Cream shantung suit—at once beautifully disciplined and utterly feminine—the first portent of a return to stricter lines." *Harper's Bazaar, March 1962*

25

26

24. COCKTAIL DRESS of black
wool with bateau neckline and
front draping; shown with black
velvet hat and black suede
shoes. Fall/Winter Collection
1962–63
Lent by Mme Emmanuel Tesch to Yves
Saint Laurent

25. DAY DRESS, two pieces, of
apricot wool flecked with gray.
Spring/Summer Collection 1963
Lent by Edward C. Blum Laboratory of
Fashion Institute of Technology

26. AFTERNOON DRESS, two
pieces, of white organdy overlaid with self-fabric cut-out leaf
motifs and floral spray appli-
qués. Spring/Summer Collection 1963
The Metropolitan Museum of Art
Gift of Mrs. Charles B. Wrightsman,
1964 (CI 64.59.7ab)

Trench Coat
Black
Gré
1962

"Style consists of very little. You don't go either too far to the left or too far to the right. The work becomes more difficult; you must be careful to reject everything that does not correspond to the style... fashion changes but style is eternal." *Yves Saint Laurent, 1972*

28

A Saint Laurent lizard boot as it appeared in *Harper's Bazaar* (September 1963) photographed by Richard Avedon

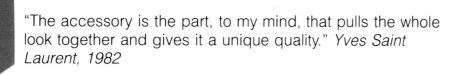

"The accessory is the part, to my mind, that pulls the whole look together and gives it a unique quality." *Yves Saint Laurent, 1982*

27. DAY DRESS of navy-blue wool with white organdy collar. Shown with white crinoline hat and navy-blue leather shoes. Spring/Summer Collection 1963
Lent by Victoire Doutreleau to Yves Saint Laurent
(Colorplate 40)

28. EVENING ENSEMBLE, coat and dress, of pearl-white silk satin. Fall/Winter Collection 1963–64
The Metropolitan Museum of Art
Gift of Mrs. Charles B. Wrightsman, 1964 (CI 64.59.2abc)

29. EVENING DRESS of purple silk crepe with sleeves of pink silk crepe beaded with rose-pink stones and embroidered with silk cord and tinsel. Fall/Winter Collection 1963–64
The Metropolitan Museum of Art
Gift of Jane Holzer, 1974 (1974.384.1)

29

38

39

39. "POLIAKOFF" COCKTAIL DRESS of red, purple, and green wool jersey; shown with black patent leather shoes with buckles. Fall/Winter Collection 1965–66

37. COCKTAIL ENSEMBLE, dress of black silk cloqué and coat of black wool overlaid with embroidered black wool cut-out flowers. Fall/Winter Collection 1965–66
The Metropolitan Museum of Art
Gift of Jane Holzer, 1977
(1977.115.17ab)

38. COCKTAIL DRESS of black velvet with pink lace petticoat and pink satin belt; shown with black suede shoes. Fall/Winter Collection 1965–66
Lent by the Musée de la Mode et du Costume, Palais Galliera, Paris, Gift of the Baronne Guy de Rothschild (E73.34.7), to Yves Saint Laurent

"My job is to work for women. Not only mannequins, beautiful women or rich women. But all women." *Yves Saint Laurent, 1982*

42. "MONDRIAN" DRESS of white, black, and red jersey; shown with black patent leather shoes with buckles. Fall/Winter Collection 1965—66
(Colorplate 55)

43. "MONDRIAN" DRESS, of white, black, red, blue, and yellow jersey; shown with black patent leather shoes with buckles. Fall/Winter Collection 1965—66
(Colorplate 55)

40. EVENING SUIT, two pieces, with jacket and knickers of rose-red velvet. Fall/Winter Collection 1965—66
The Metropolitan Museum of Art
Gift of Baron Philipe de Rothschild, 1983

41. COAT of white mink with horizontal strips of black vinyl; shown with black otter hat trimmed with white felt and black patent leather shoes with buckles. Fall/Winter Collection 1965—66

41

44

44. EVENING ENSEMBLE with overblouse embroidered in stripes of navy-blue, white, and silver sequins and pants of navy-blue silk crepe with cuffs of navy-blue sequins. Spring/Summer Collection 1966
The Metropolitan Museum of Art
Gift of Mrs. Joanne Toor Cummings, 1977 (1977.434.1ab)

45. AFTERNOON ENSEMBLE with coat and dress of beige wool; shown with black scarf with gold rings and white patent leather shoes with black heels. Spring/Summer Collection 1966
Lent by Mme Christian de Merindol to Yves Saint Laurent

46. PEACOAT of navy-blue wool twill trimmed with gold metal buttons; shown with leather cap. Spring/Summer Collection 1966
Lent by Edward C. Blum Laboratory of Fashion Institute of Technology

45

104   183   49

47. "POP ART" COCKTAIL DRESS of black, purple, blue, and red wool jersey with motif of a crescent moon; shown with bronze patent leather shoes. Fall/Winter Collection 1966–67

48. "POP ART" COCKTAIL DRESS in turquoise, navy-blue, yellow, and orange wool jersey with motif of a sun; shown with bronze patent leather shoes. Fall/Winter Collection 1966–67

49. Right: EVENING ENSEMBLE, with jacket and pants of black wool "grain de poudre," trimmed with black satin, worn with frilled blouse of white batiste and bow of black satin ribbon; shown with short black satin boots. This is the first evening ensemble created by Yves Saint Laurent in the style of men's formal evening wear. Fall/Winter Collection 1966–67
(Left and center, see nos. 104 and 183)

48

Twiggy wearing an "African" dress as it appeared in *Vogue* (March 1967) photographed by Bert Stern

50. "POP ART" DRESS of black, purple, pink, and red wool jersey with motif of a woman's face; shown with black patent leather shoes. Fall/Winter Collection 1966–67
(Colorplate 52)

51. "POP ART" DRESS of black, purple, and pink wool jersey with motif of a nude; shown with black patent leather shoes. Fall/Winter 1966–67
(Colorplate 52)

52. MINI-DRESS of dark green wool jersey trimmed with gold embroidered snake; shown with gold leather shoes. Fall/Winter Collection 1966–67
(Colorplate 31)

53. EVENING DRESS of fuchsia and yellow silk crepe; shown with shoes of matching fuchsia crepe. Spring/Summer Collection 1967
The Metropolitan Museum of Art
Gift of Lee Radziwill, 1977
(1977.157.10abc)

54. "AFRICAN" DRESS of natural wooden beads with bands of natural raffia. Spring/Summer Collection 1967
(Colorplate 11)

55. "AFRICAN" MINI-DRESS of raffia and natural wood beads embroidered with pink, black, and silver sequins. Spring/Summer Collection 1967
(Colorplate 11)

56. "AFRICAN" MINI-DRESS of brown silk appliquéd with plastic motifs and embroidered with jet, bronze-colored wooden beads, and sequins; shown with brown leather sandals. Spring/Summer Collection 1967
(Colorplates 11 and 12)

65

57. "AFRICAN" DAY ENSEMBLE with coat of red-brown raffia embroidered with beads worn over dress of natural wooden beads. Spring/Summer Collection 1967
(Colorplate 11)

58. "AFRICAN" DRESS, two pieces, of black silk crepe embroidered with black, white, and red beads of wood and glass and red and black raffia on long skirt and bandeau. Spring/Summer Collection 1967
(Colorplate 46)

59. "AFRICAN" MINI-DRESS of natural black raffia and black and red wooden beads. Spring/Summer Collection 1967
(Colorplate 46)

60. "AFRICAN" DRESS, two pieces, of glazed cotton, printed in red, green, black, purple, and yellow multicolored pattern with embroidery on skirt hip band and bandeau. Spring/Summer Collection 1967
(Colorplates 46 and 48)

53

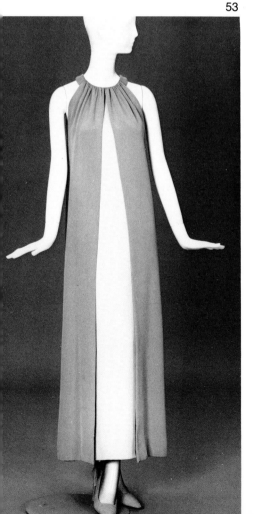

61. "AFRICAN" DRESS, two pieces, of silk printed in black, red, purple, turquoise, and brown multicolored pattern with embroidery on skirt hip band and halter top. Spring/Summer Collection 1967
(Colorplate 46)

62. "AFRICAN" EVENING DRESS of black silk organza embroidered with black wooden beads, jet beads, and appliquéd plastic geometric shapes. Spring/Summer Collection 1967
(Colorplates 56 and 57)

63. "AFRICAN" DRESS, two pieces, of black-and-white-printed silk twill, embroidered with wooden beads and trimmed with black raffia. Spring/Summer Collection 1967
(Colorplates 57 and 58)

64. "AFRICAN" EVENING DRESS, two pieces, of silk printed in multicolored pattern of green, pink, navy, red, black, and ocher, with multicolored embroidery of wood and raffia on hip band and halter top. Spring/Summer Collection 1967
(Colorplate 57)

65. EVENING DRESS completely embroidered in sequins and paillettes shaded from white through silver and gunmetal to black with lower skirt of black ostrich feathers. Fall/Winter Collection 1967–68
The Metropolitan Museum of Art
Gift of Bernice Chrysler Garbisch, 1977
(1977.108.2ab)

66. EVENING ENSEMBLE with cape and knickers of black velvet trimmed with black satin ribbons worn with blouse of white silk; shown with black patent leather shoes with buckles. Fall/Winter Collection 1967–68

67. AFTERNOON DRESS of black silk crepe with collar and cuffs of off-white satin. Fall/Winter Collection 1967–68
The Metropolitan Museum of Art
Gift of Mrs. Claus von Bulow, 1974
(1974.50.4)

67

Penelope Tree wearing one of Saint
Laurent's see-through ensembles,
photographed by Richard Avedon
for *Vogue* (March 1968)

72

68. EVENING JUMPSUIT of black silk jersey with black sequins on sleeves; shown with short boots of black patent leather. Spring/ Summer Collection 1968

69. EVENING ENSEMBLE with jacket and short pants of black wool "grain de poudre" and blouse of black silk cigaline and satin; designed in the style of men's formal evening wear; shown with shoes of black patent leather. Spring/Summer Collection 1968
(Colorplate on title page, left)

70. "SAFARI" JACKET of beige cotton worn with Bermuda shorts of black cotton and a belt of bronze rings; shown with brown felt hat with fringes of brown suede and long black suede and leather boots. July 1968
(Colorplate 47)

71. COCKTAIL DRESS, tunic-style, of brown suede embroidered with topaz rhinestones; shown with beige and brown snakeskin shoes. Fall/Winter Collection 1968–69
Gift of Mme Françoise Giroud to Yves Saint Laurent

71

72. MINI-DRESS of black silk cloqué printed in brown, green, and orange pattern with black silk fringe. Fall/Winter Collection 1968–69
Lent by Edward C. Blum Design Laboratory of Fashion Institute of Technology, Gift of Lauren Bacall
(78.257.55)

129

"I think my success depends on my ability to tune in to the life of the moment, even if I don't really live it. I have antennae, let's say, and I can accept whatever happens."
Yves Saint Laurent, 1978

A Saint Laurent suit photographed by Bill King for *Harper's Bazaar* (September 1968)

73. DAY ENSEMBLE with jacket of beige wool jersey and jumpsuit of iron-gray wool jersey; shown with black leather belt worn on head and short black patent leather boots. Fall/Winter Collection 1968–69

74. EVENING DRESS of black silk chiffon and ostrich feathers with gold "serpent" belt. Fall/Winter Collection 1968–69

77. EVENING DRESS completely embroidered with pale blue and pink beads. Spring/Summer Collection 1969
(Colorplate 44)

78. EVENING DRESS completely embroidered with pink and crystal beads. Spring/Summer Collection 1969
(Colorplate 44)

79. WEDDING DRESS of ivory silk ottoman and satin patchwork with matching belt; veil of off-white tulle and wreath of orange blossoms; shoes of white satin embroidered with pearls. Worn by H.R.H. Madame la Duchesse d'Orléans at her wedding in August 1969.
Lent by Musée de la Mode et du Costume, Palais Galliera, Paris, Gift of H.R.H. Madame la Duchesse d'Orléans (E77.60.1) to Yves Saint Laurent
(Colorplate 15)

75

75. SLIP-DRESS of white lace worn by Catherine Deneuve in *La Sirène du Mississippi*, a film directed by François Truffaut, 1969
Lent by the Musée de la Mode et du Costume, Palais Galliera, Paris, Gift of Mlle Catherine Deneuve (E77.56.1) to Yves Saint Laurent

76. PANTSUIT, safari-style, of beige wool gabardine; shown with brown leather shoes. Spring/Summer Collection 1969
Lent by Musée de la Mode et du Costume, Palais Galliera, Paris, Gift of Mme François Catroux (E77.9.1) to Yves Saint Laurent

76

Saint Laurent's belted mink coat as it appeared in *Vogue* (September 1969) photographed by Irving Penn

"I look for opposites, the unexpected—but only in materials; the style never changes." *Yves Saint Laurent, 1972*

81

82

80. EVENING DRESS of Bird of Paradise feathers. Fall/Winter Collection 1969–70
The Metropolitan Museum of Art
Gift of Baron Philippe de Rothschild, 1983

81. EVENING SUIT, two pieces, with tunic and hotpants of brown organza embroidered with purple beads and sequins. Fall/Winter Collection 1969–70

82. EVENING DRESS of Bird of Paradise feathers. Fall/Winter Collection 1969–70

83. COAT of black and white ermine, otter, and astrakhan furs in patchwork pattern worn over tunic of black wool jersey; shown with hat of white knitted wool and thigh-high boots of black leather. Fall/Winter Collection 1969–70

84. EVENING DRESS of black ostrich and brown cock feathers. Fall/Winter Collection 1969–70

84

83

A Saint Laurent coat photographed
by Neal Barr for *Harper's Bazaar*
(September 1969)

85. DRESS of brown crushed velvet trimmed with brown cock feathers; shown with brown satin shoes. Fall/Winter Collection 1969—70

86. EVENING DRESS of black silk crepe georgette with matching stole and Claude Lalanne body sculpture of golden-galvanized copper. Fall/Winter Collection 1969—70
(Colorplates 59 and 60)

87. EVENING DRESS of blue silk crepe georgette with matching stole and Claude Lalanne body sculpture of golden-galvanized copper. Fall/Winter Collection 1969—70
(Colorplates 59 and 60)

88. Left: THEATRICAL COSTUME, mini-coat of black and white zebra-patterned sequins trimmed with black fox, worn by Zizi Jeanmaire at the Casino de Paris, 1970
Lent by Mlle Zizi Jeanmaire to Yves Saint Laurent
(Right, see no. 100)

89. THEATRICAL CAPE of black and white ostrich feathers, worn by Zizi Jeanmaire at the Casino de Paris, 1970
Lent by Mlle Zizi Jeanmaire to Yves Saint Laurent
(Colorplate 1)

90

85

90. DAY ENSEMBLE with jacket of beige wool gabardine, pants of black wool "grain de poudre," and blouse of black silk, shown with red, beige, and black wool scarf, beige felt hat and black patent leather shoes with straps. Spring/Summer Collection 1970

91. COCKTAIL DRESS of black crepe and black velvet, shown with black satin shoes. Fall/Winter Collection 1970–71

92. EVENING PANTSUIT with tunic overblouse of green satin trimmed with magenta and violet, worn with pants of black satin embroidered with multicolored butterflies and flowers. Fall/Winter Collection 1970–71
The Metropolitan Museum of Art
Gift of Bernice Chrysler Garbisch, 1978
(1978.34.5ab)

93. COAT of black, white, and brown wool plaid trimmed with black passementerie. Fall/Winter 1970–71
Lent by Mirielle Levy

A Saint Laurent
evening ensemble
photographed by
Neal Barr for
Harper's Bazaar
(September 1970)

141

94. COCKTAIL DRESS of black silk crepe with back of black lace; shown with black velvet turban and black suede platform shoes. Fall/Winter Collection 1970–71
Lent by the Musée de la Mode et du Costume, Palais Galliera, Paris, Gift of Mme François Catroux (E.77.9.6), to Yves Saint Laurent
(Colorplate 6)

95. DAY ENSEMBLE with coat of burgundy, brown, and black suede over dress of blue-green crushed velvet; shown with brown felt hat trimmed with pheasant feathers and burgundy suede boots with gold nails. Fall/Winter Collection 1970–71
Dress lent by Mme José Muñoz-Yagué to Yves Saint Laurent
(Colorplate 53)

96. COAT of rust-colored suede with beige, ocher, green, brown, and navy multicolored suede patches worn over dress of multicolored crepe; shown with brown felt hat and laced boots of ocher and green leather. Fall/Winter Collection 1970–71
Dress lent by Mme José Muñoz-Yagué to Yves Saint Laurent
(Colorplate 53)

97. COCKTAIL ENSEMBLE with bolero of silver fox and dress of black silk jersey; shown with purple velvet turban and black suede platform sandals. Spring/Summer Collection 1971

98. MINI-COAT of green fox; shown with black velvet turban and black patent leather sandals. Spring/Summer Collection 1971
(Colorplate 28)

99. THEATRICAL COSTUME, with tailcoat and pants of black wool "grain de poudre," worn by Zizi Jeanmaire at the Casino de Paris, 1972
Lent by Mlle Zizi Jeanmaire to Yves Saint Laurent

97

100. Right in fig. no. 88: THEATRICAL COSTUME, coat completely embroidered in white sequins with white fox collar, worn by Zizi Jeanmaire at the Casino de Paris, 1972.
Lent by Mlle Zizi Jeanmaire to Yves Saint Laurent

101. EVENING JACKET of black quilted silk ciré trimmed with dark brown sable and belt of black patent leather; shown with black skirt. Fall/Winter Collection 1972–73
The Metropolitan Museum of Art Gift of Lauren Bacall, 1979 (1972. 73)

102. EVENING DRESS of taupe chiffon, trimmed with white-and-brown-striped ostrich feathers. Fall/Winter Collection 1973–74
The Metropolitan Museum of Art
Gift of Mrs. Charles Wrightsman, 1976
(1976.237ab)

103. SWEATER, cardigan-style, embroidered with pearls and pale yellow rhinestones. Spring/Summer Collection 1974

103

104. Left in fig. no. 49: JUMPSUIT of black wool gabardine designed in the style of men's formal wear; shown with black satin evening sandals. Spring/ Summer Collection 1975

105. EVENING DRESS of tobacco-colored silk crepe georgette with matching scarf; shown with brown satin and bronze leather sandals. Spring/Summer Collection 1975

105

106. SUIT of khaki and beige wool tweed with blouse of silk crepe de chine printed in tweed pattern; shown with beige felt hat and brown lizard sandals. Fall/Winter Collection 1975–76
Lent by Mme José Muñoz-Yagué to Yves Saint Laurent

107. EVENING DRESS of silver-gray panné velvet mottled in pale blue-gray. Fall/Winter Collection 1975–76
The Metropolitan Museum of Art Gift of Mrs. Charles B. Wrightsman, 1978 (1978.177.)

108. EVENING DRESS of dark gray silk chiffon trimmed with mauve silk ribbon. Fall/Winter Collection 1975–76
The Metropolitan Museum of Art Gift of Mrs. Charles B. Wrightsman, 1983. (1983.296.1ab)

107

108

109. "RUSSIAN" DAY ENSEMBLE, three pieces, with coat of gray suede lined with beaver, skirt of purple wool broadcloth, and tunic of blue open-weave wool; shown with black fox hat and brown suede boots. Fall/Winter Collection 1976–77

110. "RUSSIAN" EVENING DRESS of black velvet and fuchsia faille embroidered with jet; shown with black chiffon turban and black satin sandals with laces. Fall/Winter Collection 1976–77
(Colorplate 19)

112. "RUSSIAN" EVENING EN-SEMBLE, three pieces, with bolero of red velvet embroidered with jet, skirt of black moiré and red velvet embroidered with jet and black tassels, and blouse of black chiffon; shown with black satin turban and black satin sandals with laces. Fall/Winter Collection 1976–77
(Colorplate 19)

111. "RUSSIAN" EVENING EN-SEMBLE, three pieces, with vest of emerald-green velvet trimmed with sable, skirt of Prussian-blue ottoman, blouse of bright blue and metallic gold chiffon; shown with blue, green, and gold turban and silver-and-gold lizard sandals. Fall/Winter Collection 1976–77
(Colorplate 19)

Saint Laurent's drawings for the Fall/Winter 1976–77 collection

113. "RUSSIAN" EVENING DRESS with bodice of black velvet, sleeves of orange satin, skirt of pale green satin trimmed with claret velvet, fuchsia satin ribbon at waist; shown with multicolored printed velvet turban and bronze leather sandals. Fall/Winter Collection 1976–77
(Colorplate 19)

114. "RUSSIAN" EVENING DRESS, two pieces, with corselet-style bodice of black velvet and satin and full skirt of yellow satin; shown with black-and-gold turban and gold leather sandals. Fall/Winter Collection 1976–77
(Colorplate 19)

115. "RUSSIAN" EVENING EN-SEMBLE, three pieces, with vest of purple velvet trimmed with sable, skirt of green faille, and blouse of purple and gold chiffon; shown with multicolored lamé turban and gold leather shoes. Fall/Winter Collection 1976–77
(Colorplate 19)

120. "SPANISH" DAY ENSEMBLE, two pieces, with corselet bodice of black moiré and white cotton Bermuda shorts; shown with black lace mantilla with multicolored fringe and black satin sandals with red satin ruffle. Spring/Summer Collection 1977
(Colorplate 30)

118   119

116. EVENING ENSEMBLE with coat of gold lamé embroidered with jet and trimmed with black mink worn over skirt of black velvet; shown with black bear-fur hat and gold leather boots. Fall/Winter Collection 1976–77
(Colorplate 20)

117. "SPANISH" DAY ENSEMBLE, three pieces, with jacket of off-white wool flannel trimmed with ivory passementerie, pants of beige wool gabardine, and blouse of ivory silk crepe de chine; shown with natural straw hat trimmed with white passementerie and tassels and beige crocodile shoes. Spring/Summer Collection 1977

118. "SPANISH" EVENING ENSEMBLE with corselet bodice of black moiré and skirt of hot-pink lamé taffeta; shown with black velvet hat trimmed with pink feathers and black satin sandals. Spring/Summer Collection 1977

119. "SPANISH" EVENING DRESS of black lace and taffeta; shown with black satin sandals with tassels. Spring/Summer Collection 1977

121. EVENING ENSEMBLE, two pieces, with blouse of white chiffon and white lace, skirt of emerald-green moiré; shown with natural straw hat trimmed with white flowers and ivory satin sandals trimmed with gold leather. Spring/Summer Collection 1977
(Colorplates 13 and 14)

122. EVENING ENSEMBLE, three pieces, with short quilted jacket of black shantung printed in ivory and green, skirt of emerald-green faille, and blouse of white textured chiffon; shown with white straw hat trimmed with white flowers and black satin sandals. Spring/Summer Collection 1977
(Colorplate 14)

123. EVENING DRESS of white Chantilly lace and white bobbin lace trimmed with black velvet ribbons; shown with white straw hat trimmed with white flowers and black ribbon, and white satin sandals with white leather laces. Spring/Summer Collection 1977
(Colorplate 14)

126

124. "CHINESE" EVENING EN-
SEMBLE, three pieces, with
coat of black velvet embroidered with gold, pants of black
silk ciré, and blouse of black-
and-gold chiffon; shown with
gold silk ciré hat bordered
with mink and black satin
sandals with gold laces and
heels. Fall/Winter Collection
1977–78

125. "CHINESE" EVENING EN-
SEMBLE, three pieces, with
coat of black silk ciré embroidered with gold sequins
and trimmed with black mink,
pants of purple satin trimmed
with gold-and-black tassels,
and bodice of knitted gold
jersey; shown with black
leather boots trimmed with
black mink. Fall/Winter Collection 1977–78

126. EVENING JACKET of quilted
red satin trimmed with gold
satin. Fall/Winter Collection
1977–78

127. DAY ENSEMBLE, three
pieces, with double cape of
black velvet trimmed with
white fox, pants of black velvet trimmed with dark mink,
and pullover of black wool;
shown with black velvet skullcap trimmed with black passementerie and black suede
boots with passementerie
laces. Fall/Winter Collection
1977–78

127

128. "CHINESE" EVENING EN-
SEMBLE, three pieces, with
coat of shocking pink and
gold brocade, pants of red
velvet, and blouse of fuchsia
crepe; shown with fuchsia
satin and red velvet hat
trimmed with pink flowers and
feathers and burgundy suede
boots with tassels. Fall/Win-
ter Collection 1977–78
(Colorplate 26)

129. "CHINESE" EVENING EN-
SEMBLE, two pieces, with

jacket of black and red silk
ciré and pants of black velvet; shown with red silk ciré
and black velvet hat and
black suede boots trimmed
with fur. Fall/Winter Collection 1977–78
(Colorplate 26)

130. "CHINESE" EVENING EN-
SEMBLE, three pieces, with
coat of red, black, and gold
brocade trimmed with black
fox, pants of black velvet, and
blouse of rust-colored satin

crepe; shown with brown velvet "Miller's" cap trimmed with
passementerie tassels and
black suede boots trimmed
with fox fur and corded lac-
ings. Fall/Winter Collection
1977–78
(Colorplate 26)

131. "CHINESE" EVENING EN-
SEMBLE, two pieces, with
coat of gold damask and
pants of quilted black velvet;
shown with black vinyl headband and black velvet boots
with gold heels and black and
gold passementerie. Fall/
Winter Collection 1977–78
(Colorplate 26)

132. "CHINESE" EVENING EN-
SEMBLE, two pieces, with
coat of black, gold, and purple brocade and pants of
purple silk damask; shown
with gold damask hat trimmed
with ceramic flowers and
black suede boots trimmed
with gold leather. Fall/Winter
Collection 1977–78
(Colorplate 26)

133. EVENING DRESS of black
velvet trimmed with green and
bronze taffeta ruffles; shown
with brown satin shoes with
bronze laces. Fall/Winter Collection 1977–78
(Colorplate 2)

134. EVENING DRESS of brown silk
chiffon printed in smoke patterns; shown with brown satin
sandals with bronze leather
shoelaces. Fall/Winter Collection 1977–78
(Colorplate 5)

134a. PANTSUIT with jacket and
pants of gray-green wool herringbone and blouse of gray
crepe de chine shown with
chiffon scarf in shades of
gray, beige, and white, and
with brown lizard shoes.
Spring/Summer Collection
1978
Lent by Louise de la Falaise to Yves
Saint Laurent

135. PANTSUIT with jacket and pants of light pink wool herringbone and blouse of pink crepe de chine; shown with silver straw boater trimmed with pink and blue plaid ribbon and pink leather shoes. Spring/Summer Collection 1978
(Colorplate 23)

136. THEATRICAL DRESS of blue, purple, and brown iridescent taffeta, worn by Genevieve Page as the Queen in *L'Aigle a deux têtes* by Jean Cocteau at the Théâtre de l'Athénée—Louis Jouvet, 1978. Shown with a black tulle veil and purple velvet shoes

137

137. EVENING JACKET of black velvet embroidered with multicolored dots. Fall/Winter Collection 1978–79
Lent by Louise de la Falaise to Yves Saint Laurent

138. DAY ENSEMBLE, four pieces, with coat and jacket of black, blue, and beige wool tartan, skirt of black wool, and blouse of printed black, brown, blue, and white crepe de chine; shown with blue felt hat, mustard-colored silk scarf, and navy-blue crocodile shoes. Fall/Winter Collection 1978–79

138

"Although I have no ideal woman, perhaps I have an ideal of a lifestyle that is really *passéiste*—the way people used to live in the past. For me, the greatest years were between the end of World War I and the beginning of World War II. These years are my inspiration; they continue to vibrate in all the arts." *Yves Saint Laurent, 1978*

165   139

139. Right: EVENING DRESS of gold lamé trimmed with black velvet bows; shown with black satin and gold leather sandals. Fall/Winter Collection 1978–79
(Left: see no. 165.)

"When it's pants, it's Yves Saint Laurent!" *Lauren Bacall, 1977*

140

142. "SPANISH" EVENING EN-
SEMBLE, two pieces, with
cape of pink gazar and dress
of black velvet and pink gazar; shown with black velvet
headband with pink and
fuchsia sequined orchids,
necklace of black passe-
menterie trimmed with jet and
red stones, and black satin
sandals with laces. Fall/Win-
ter Collection 1979–80

1

140. DAY ENSEMBLE, three
pieces, with jacket of ocher
linen, pants of brown shantung, and blouse of sand-col-
ored shantung; shown with
natural straw hat trimmed with
brown grosgrain ribbon and
brown lizard shoes. Spring/
Summer Collection 1979

141. DAY ENSEMBLE, two pieces,
with tunic and pants of black
silk jersey; shown with black
sequined skullcap and black
satin sandals with rhinestone
and jet buckles. Spring/Sum-
mer Collection 1979

141

145. DRESS of black velvet; shown with black silk velvet hat with black feathers and black satin shoes. Fall/Winter Collection 1979–80

146. EVENING DRESS of black and white satin crepe; shown with black sequined cap trimmed with black velvet and black satin sandals with laces. Fall/Winter Collection 1979–80

145

143. "HARLEQUIN" DRESS of satin patchwork in pastel colors trimmed with black tulle; shown with black velvet hat with pink and black feathers and black patent leather shoes. Fall/Winter Collection 1979–80

144. "HARLEQUIN BOY" ENSEMBLE, two pieces, with jacket and pants of satin patchwork in pastel colors trimmed with white tulle; shown with black velvet hat and black patent leather shoes. Fall/Winter Collection 1979–80

3   144

146

147. CAPE of dark red mohair trimmed with marmot and nutria fur. Fall/Winter Collection 1979–80

148. "SPANISH" DAY ENSEMBLE, three pieces, with coat of gray wool, skirt of brown velvet, and blouse of brown satin and velvet; shown with brown velvet toreador-style hat and brown suede and leather shoes. Fall/Winter Collection 1979–80

149. CAPE of black mohair trimmed with black fox and red mink fur. Fall/Winter Collection 1979–80

147

148

150. "PICASSO" SUIT, three pieces, with jacket of blue, turquoise, and yellow broadcloth, skirt of blue-and-black checked wool, and sleeveless top of black velvet; shown with green-and-yellow velvet turban and black lizard shoes. Fall/Winter Collection 1979–80
(Colorplate 16)

151. EVENING JACKET of red velvet embroidered in gold and burgundy. Fall/Winter Collection 1979–80
(Colorplate 22)

152. "PICASSO" DRESS of black satin embroidered with light yellow and pink sequins in motif of a face; shown with black velvet hat with gold metal leaves and pink feathers and black satin sandals with bow of black tulle. Fall/Winter Collection 1979–80
(Colorplate 49)

153. EVENING ENSEMBLE, three pieces, with toreador jacket and breeches of gold lamé brocade and black velvet, skirt of "Goya-green" moiré, and blouse of black chiffon dotted with gold; shown with black velvet satin hat and black satin sandals. Fall/Winter Collection 1979–80
(Colorplate 38)

1

157. JACKET of blue flannel trimmed with gold-and-red braid and black passementerie. Spring/Summer Collection 1980

158. EVENING DRESS of black gazar with flounces; shown with bronze-and-gold leather sandals. Spring/Summer Collection 1980

154. DAYTIME ENSEMBLE, four pieces, with cape of sapphire-blue mohair, jacket of black wool, short "zouave" pants of dark red velvet, and sleeveless top of black velvet; shown with red felt fez and burgundy suede shoes. Fall/Winter Collection 1979–80
(Colorplate 29)

155. "PICASSO" EVENING DRESS of orange moiré with multi-colored satin appliqué on skirt; shown with green felt hat trimmed with pink tulle and sequined cockade and black satin sandals. Fall/Winter Collection 1979–80
(Colorplates 33 and 34)

156. COCKTAIL SUIT with jacket and skirt of black wool "grain de poudre" and blouse of black-and-yellow-striped satin crepe; shown with gold-and-black straw hat and black ottoman shoes. Spring/Summer Collection 1980

158

161. EVENING ENSEMBLE, two pieces, with dress of black purple, and orange lace in patchwork pattern, and jacket of black chiffon and marabou; shown with mauve tulle headdress and black satin sandals. Spring/Summer Collection 1980
(Colorplates 3 and 4)

162. DAY ENSEMBLE, four pieces, with tunic of red wool jersey and skirt of black wool jersey, scarf of black fox and red mink fur, and muff of black fox; shown with black velvet beret and shoes of black leather. Fall/Winter Collection 1980–81
Lent by the Baroness de Ludinghausen to Yves Saint Laurent

159. "MONDRIAN" SUIT, three pieces, with jacket of white, red, blue, yellow, and black linen, skirt of black gabardine, and top of black and white linen; shown with glossy black straw hat and black patent leather shoes. Spring/Summer Collection 1980

160. EVENING JACKET of black gazar embroidered with gold oak leaves. Spring/Summer Collection 1980

160

163. EVENING ENSEMBLE, three pieces, with trenchcoat of gold leather, skirt of black velvet, and tunic of gold lamé; shown with black velvet beret and black suede shoes. Fall/Winter Collection 1980–81

164. EVENING ENSEMBLE, two pieces, with coat of gold leather embroidered with multicolored flowers and dress of emerald-green velvet and satin; shown with black velvet and fur hat with mauve chiffon scarf and black satin and gold leather sandals. Fall/Winter Collection 1980–81

165. Left in fig. no. 139: EVENING DRESS of gold figured lamé trimmed with black velvet bow; shown with black fox stole and black satin sandals. Fall/Winter Collection 1980–81

166. DAYTIME ENSEMBLE, four pieces, with jacket of black and white Prince of Wales wool, kilt of red plaid wool, blouse of green silk damask, and shawl of black and white plaid wool trimmed with black leather fringe; shown with green velvet beret trimmed with black ostrich feather, gold and pearl brooch, and brown leather shoes. Fall/Winter Collection 1980–81
(Colorplate 42)

167. DAY ENSEMBLE, two pieces, with coat of camel cashmere and dress of brown ribbed silk jersey; shown with man's hat of brown felt trimmed with brown grosgrain and brown leather shoes. Fall/Winter Collection 1980–81
(Colorplate 9)

170. WEDDING DRESS, two pieces, with cape of gold and orange brocade and dress of gold damask, shown with gold lamé headdress with veil of black-and-gold point d'esprit and gold lizard shoes. Fall/Winter Collection 1980–81
(Colorplate 39)

171. EVENING DRESS of black lace re-embroidered with gold; shown with black tulle veil and black crepe sandals. Fall/Winter Collection 1980–81

168. "SHAKESPEARE" SUIT, three pieces, with jacket and skirt of burgundy velvet and blouse of burgundy-and-gold lace, shown with burgundy velvet beret trimmed with blue ostrich feathers and burgundy velvet shoes embroidered with red pearls and stones. Fall/Winter Collection 1980–81
(Colorplates 50 and 51)

169. EVENING JACKET of pink satin, embroidered with a line from "Batterie" by Jean Cocteau. Fall/Winter Collection 1980–81
(Colorplate 54)

171

172. CEREMONIAL UNIFORM designed for Marguerite Yourcenar to wear for her induction into the Académie Française, January 1981. Cape of black wool, jacket, skirt, and belt of black velvet trimmed with black passementerie, and blouse of white crepe; shown with white chiffon and satin scarf.

173. DAY ENSEMBLE, three pieces, with jacket of black flannel, skirt and tunic of black pin-striped wool with black trim; shown with natural straw hat trimmed with black grosgrain ribbon and black leather shoes. Spring/Summer Collection 1981

174. DAY ENSEMBLE, three pieces, with coat of light brown leather, pants of dark brown leather, and blouse of light brown and black silk; shown with glossy black straw hat trimmed with black grosgrain ribbon and light brown lizard shoes. Spring/Summer Collection 1981

175. DAY DRESS of navy-blue wool with white batiste collar and cuffs and white batiste and navy-blue silk bow; shown with navy-blue straw boater with veil and navy-blue lizard and leather shoes. Spring/Summer Collection 1981

176. WEDDING DRESS, two pieces, of beige organdy woven with gold; shown with gold straw hat with gold and white tulle trimmed with a velvet bow and white flowers and a matching organdy sunshade. Spring/Summer Collection 1981

177. EVENING ENSEMBLE, two pieces, with tunic and full skirt of black satin with matching stole; shown with black satin shoes trimmed with rhinestones. Spring/Summer Collection 1981

178. COCKTAIL SUIT with jacket of black and white ottoman, skirt of black wool "grain de poudre," and blouse of white and black silk organdy; shown with glossy black straw boater with veil and black lizard and patent shoes. Spring/Summer Collection 1981
(Colorplates 36 and 37)

179. EVENING DRESS of red-orange silk organdy woven with gold; shown with shoes of gold and silver lizard. Spring/Summer Collection 1981
(Colorplate 8)

176   177

"Classics are something you can wear all your life. I do classic things for women to have the same assurance with their clothes that men have with theirs." *Yves Saint Laurent, 1982*

181

180. EVENING GOWN of iridescent purple faille; shown with
black ostrich-feather head-
dress and purple satin shoes
topstitched with gold. Fall/
Winter Collection 1981–82
(Right, see no. 207)

181. PANTSUIT with jacket of yellow wool, pants of black flannel, and blouse of black satin;
shown with black velvet beret
trimmed with black passe-
menterie and black suede
shoes. Fall/Winter Collection
1981–82

182. EVENING DRESS of black
satin and white taffeta; shown
with black satin open-toe
slippers trimmed with rhinestones. Fall/Winter Collection
1981–82

183. Center in fig. no. 49: EVE-
NING SUIT with peacoat-style
jacket of black wool and satin,
skirt of black wool "grain de
poudre," and sweater of black
silk jersey, designed in the
style of men's formal evening
wear; shown with draped
black crepe shoes. Fall/Win-
ter Collection 1981–82

182

184. EVENING JACKET of white satin appliquéd in black velvet with jet beading, and collar of black fox. Fall/Winter Collection 1981–82

185. EVENING SUIT, two pieces, with jacket and skirt embroidered with gold and multicolored rhinestones; shown with black aigrette headdress and gold leather sandals. Fall/Winter Collection 1981–82

186. SUIT with jacket of pearl-grey broadcloth embroidered with black jet and pants of black wool "grain de poudre"; shown with black felt fez and black suede shoes. Fall/Winter Collection 1981–82

187. SUIT with jacket and skirt of gray wool whipcord and blouse of silver-gray satin; shown with gray fox scarf, gray felt hat, and gray suede shoes. Fall/Winter Collection 1981–82
(Colorplate 35)

188. COCKTAIL DRESS of steel-gray taffeta; shown with black satin shoes trimmed with rhinestones. Fall/Winter Collection 1981–82
(Colorplate 27)

185

186

EVENING SUIT with bolero jacket and skirt of black grosgrain embroidered with black, red, and yellow sequins, and sleeveless blouse of black chiffon embroidered with black sequins; shown with orange shantung turban and black grosgrain shoes. Spring/Summer Collection 1982

189. COCKTAIL DRESS of shocking-pink taffeta; shown with black satin shoes trimmed with rhinestones. Fall/Winter Collection 1981–82 (Colorplate 27)

190. "MATISSE" EVENING DRESS of blue and white taffeta; shown with blue satin shoes topstitched in gold. Fall/Winter Collection 1981–82 (Colorplate 7)

191. EVENING ENSEMBLE, two pieces, with tunic of ivory shantung embroidered with gold and white pearls, and skirt of black shantung; shown with beige lizard shoes trimmed with white leather. Spring/Summer Collection 1982

192

193. DAYTIME ENSEMBLE, three pieces, with spencer jacket of black gabardine, pants of black and white houndstooth-check wool, and blouse of white crepe de chine with black polka dots; shown with black-striped natural straw hat and black patent leather shoes trimmed with white leather. Spring/Summer Collection 1982

198

194. DAY ENSEMBLE, three pieces, with bolero of black grosgrain, skirt of black pin-striped wool, and blouse of white shantung with black satin bow; shown with black-striped straw hat trimmed with black velvet ribbon and black crepe shoes. Spring/Summer Collection 1982
(Colorplate 24)

195. DAY DRESS of black gabardine and white piqué; shown with white and black straw hat trimmed with white grosgrain ribbon, and black leather shoes trimmed with black patent and white leather. Spring/Summer Collection 1982
(Colorplate 41)

196. EVENING SUIT with spencer jacket and pants of black wool "grain de poudre" and blouse of white crepe, designed in the style of men's formal evening wear; shown with black crepe shoes with rhinestones. Spring/Summer Collection 1982
(Colorplate on title page, right)

197. EVENING GOWN of black tulle embroidered with jet; shown with black egret-feather head-dress and black satin sandals. Fall/Winter Collection 1982–83

198. SUIT with jacket and skirt of grey wool herringbone and blouse of plaid satin crepe; shown with black felt hat with bow of black velvet. Fall/ Winter Collection 1982–83

199. EVENING DRESS of sapphire and amethyst leopard-printed satin crepe; shown with black crepe sandals. Fall/Winter Collection 1982–83

199

200

201

200. EVENING SUIT with bolero jacket of dark red velvet, skirt of red and black velvet, and blouse of fuchsia satin; shown with fuchsia felt hat trimmed with bow of black velvet and black crepe shoes. Fall/Winter Collection 1982–83

201. SUIT with jacket and skirt of dark blue leather and blouse of black and purple figured taffeta; shown with purple felt hat trimmed with black ribbon and blue suede shoes. Fall/Winter Collection 1982–83

202. EVENING DRESS, two pieces, of black velvet and white crepe; shown with black satin sandals trimmed with rhinestones. Fall/Winter Collection 1982–83
(Colorplate 10)

203. DAYTIME ENSEMBLE, three pieces, with jacket of beige and khaki Prince of Wales wool, skirt of beige and khaki houndstooth-check wool, and blouse of yellow-and-brown plaid silk crepe; shown with green and brown lizard hat trimmed with black velvet ribbon and veil and beige suede shoes with topstitching. Fall/Winter Collection 1982–83
(Colorplate 17)

204. EVENING DRESS completely embroidered with silver and turquoise sequined scales; shown with black satin shoes trimmed with rhinestones. Spring/Summer Collection 1983

205. SUIT with jacket and skirt of black and white pinstriped wool and blouse of black and white satin; shown with glossy black straw boater trimmed with white ribbon and black python shoes. Spring/ Summer Collection 1983

206. COCKTAIL DRESS of black crepe; shown with black crepe sandals trimmed with rhinestones. Spring/Summer Collection 1983

210. DAYTIME ENSEMBLE, two pieces, with jacket of pink linen and dress of pink and green printed crepe; shown with purple straw hat trimmed with dark blue ribbon and shoes of matching crepe. Spring/Summer Collection 1983

211. DAYTIME ENSEMBLE, three pieces, with jacket and skirt of black and white hounds-tooth-check wool and blouse of blue and white dotted crepe de chine; shown with black and white straw hat trimmed with a black satin ribbon and black lizard shoes. Spring/Summer Collection 1983

207. EVENING DRESS of black satin; shown with black crinoline-and-feather head-dress and black crepe shoes trimmed with rhine-stones. Spring/Summer Collection 1983
(See fig. no. 180)

208. DAY DRESS of light blue linen; shown with light blue felt hat trimmed with black ribbon and beige python sandals. Spring/Summer Collection 1983

209. AFTERNOON ENSEMBLE, two pieces, with tunic of black crepe with white dots and skirt of black ottoman; shown with black straw hat trimmed with white camelia and black crepe shoes. Spring/Summer Collection 1983

212. EVENING DRESS, two pieces, with tunic of white crepe embroidered with jet and pearls and skirt of black crepe; shown with black crinoline bow trimmed with black feathers and rhinestones and black crepe shoes trimmed with rhinestones. Spring/Summer Collection 1983

213. EVENING JACKET entirely embroidered with crystal and rhinestone beads; shown with gray flannel pants and white mousseline blouse, to represent the look of 1973. Spring/Summer Collection 1983 (Colorplate 32)

214. DAY ENSEMBLE with coat of black wool and chemise dress of cobalt-blue jersey; shown with black suede gloves and black felt capeline with black ribbon, and black python shoes. Fall/Winter Collection 1983–84

215. COCKTAIL DRESS of black velvet; shown with black velvet shoes. Fall/Winter Collection 1983–84

"Luxury is above all an attitude of the heart. I never considered it as something that revolves around money, jewels, or furs; it's mostly a respect for others that makes someone luxurious in their gestures, in their attitudes. Luxury is something interior which is translated in external terms. The biggest luxury in life is to love others and to understand them, whatever level they may be on." *Yves Saint Laurent, 1978*

216. DAY DRESS of figured satin crepe printed with red and purple; shown with head-piece of two red flowers with red and purple sequins and red crepe shoes. Fall/Winter Collection 1983–84

217. EVENING DRESS of black lamé and crushed velvet; shown with black crepe shoes with rhinestone button. Fall/Winter Collection 1983–84

218. EVENING ENSEMBLE with cape of yellow silk faille and dress of black velvet and lace; shown with black crepe shoes with rhinestone button. Fall/Winter Collection 1983–84

217

Staff of the Costume Institute

Diana Vreeland, Special Consultant
K. Gordon Stone, Associate Museum Librarian
Jean R. Druesedow, Assistant Curator
Paul M. Ettesvold, Assistant Curator
Judith Jerde, Assistant Conservator
Lillian A. Dickler, Senior Administrative Assistant
Patricia Lennox, Senior Administrative Assistant
Mary Martinez, Senior Housekeeper
Dominick Tallarico, Principal Departmental Technician
Mavis Dalton, Associate Curator, part-time

Exhibition conceived and organized by Diana Vreeland
Assistant to Mrs. Vreeland: Stephen Jamail
Assistant to Mr. Saint Laurent for the exhibition: Stephen de Pietri
Exhibition assistants: Katell le Bourhis, Richard DeGussi-Bogutski, Sarah Richardson
Designers: Jeffrey Daly, David Harvey
Lighting: William L. Riegel
Mannequins by SCHLÄPPI

Acknowledgments: The Publishers would like to thank the following individuals who were very helpful in the preparation of this book: Veronique Benard, Gabrielle Buchaert, Marina Daumain, Louise de la Falaise, Christophe Girard, Anne-Marie Muñoz-Yagué, Hector Pascual, and Myriam Rollin of the house of Yves Saint Laurent; the photographers Richard Avedon, Irving Penn, Bill King, Bert Stern, and Neal Barr for their permission to reproduce photographs; Diana Edkins and Cynthia Cathcart of Condé Nast; Myrna Borsuk of Harper's Bazaar; and Nina Hyde of the *Washington Post*. The Editor would like to give a special note of thanks to Andrew Solomon for his assistance on all aspects of this project.